American Literature:
Poe Through Garland

GOLDENTREE BIBLIOGRAPHIES IN LANGUAGE AND LITERATURE

under the series editorship of O. B. HARDISON, JR.

LINGUISTICS AND ENGLISH LINGUISTICS • Harold B. Allen

OLD AND MIDDLE ENGLISH LITERATURE • William Matthews

CHAUCER • Albert C. Baugh

THE SIXTEENTH CENTURY: SKELTON THROUGH HOOKER •
John L. Lievsay

SHAKESPEARE: COMEDIES AND SONNETS • James G. McManaway
& Jeanne A. Roberts

SHAKESPEARE: TRAGEDIES AND HISTORIES • James G. McManaway
& Jeanne A. Roberts

TUDOR AND STUART DRAMA • Irving Ribner

THE SEVENTEENTH CENTURY: BACON THROUGH MARVELL •
Arthur E. Barker

MILTON • James Holly Hanford

THE AGE OF DRYDEN • Donald F. Bond

THE EIGHTEENTH CENTURY • Donald F. Bond

ROMANTIC POETS AND PROSE WRITERS • Richard Harter Fogle

VICTORIAN POETS AND PROSE WRITERS • Jerome H. Buckley

THE BRITISH NOVEL THROUGH JANE AUSTEN • Wayne C. Booth
& Gwin J. Kolb

THE BRITISH NOVEL: SCOTT THROUGH HARDY • Ian P. Watt

THE BRITISH NOVEL: CONRAD TO THE PRESENT • Paul L. Wiley

AFRO-AMERICAN WRITERS • Darwin T. Turner

AMERICAN LITERATURE THROUGH BRYANT • Richard Beale Davis

AMERICAN LITERATURE: POE THROUGH GARLAND • Harry Hayden Clark

AMERICAN DRAMA FROM ITS BEGINNINGS TO THE PRESENT •
E. Hudson Long

THE AMERICAN NOVEL THROUGH HENRY JAMES • C. Hugh Holman

THE AMERICAN NOVEL: SINCLAIR LEWIS TO THE PRESENT •
Blake Nevius

LITERARY CRITICISM: PLATO THROUGH JOHNSON • Vernon Hall

American Literature: Poe Through Garland

compiled by

Harry Hayden Clark

The University of Wisconsin

APPLETON-CENTURY-CROFTS

Educational Division

New York   MEREDITH CORPORATION

Carpenter
Z
1227
.C58

PRINTED IN THE UNITED STATES OF AMERICA

cloth: 390-19324-0
paper: 390-19323-2

Preface

SINCE THE NOVEL and the drama have been covered by others in the Goldentree series, the present bibliography, dealing with the authors whose work reached a peak between 1830 and 1914, will emphasize the writers' contribution to the short story, literary theory and criticism, social or travel commentary, history, and letters. The last quarter of a century has witnessed an especially stimulating development of literary interpretation, including "The New Criticism." At its best the latter has tried to look at a poem or story itself, just as one looks at a painting, trying to find patterns, high-lights, contrasts, etc., without speculating too much on peculiarities of the author's or painter's personal life. But I have included the best biographies that help one to understand why a given author, conditioned by heredity and environment and a special sequence of readings, was led to produce his distinctive writings, influenced by various turning-points in his life. Studies have been included which enable the reader to visualize a given story or poem as part of an historical trend or to view the author, when the facts warrant, as a spokesman of some aspects of his era. And a balance has been sought between studies of technique and studies in the meaning of the literature involved, for as an ultimate end it is assumed that literature has significance in proportion as one focuses his inquiry on its beauty and its wisdom associated with the conduct of life.

This compilation, intermediate between the huge non-selective book-length bibliographies of individual authors and the anthology "reading lists" limited to six or seven items, has been especially designed to help students who are trying to write reports and "term papers," to prepare for exams, and to do independent reading. Even in one year nearly a thousand studies are now printed on some of our major American authors. Hence a student especially needs guidance in selecting studies of sterling value. The section on Bibliographical References including aids such as the annual "MLA International Bibliography," should help the student keep abreast of further or more extended studies. Attention is called to four features intended to enhance the utility of this Bibliography for the period from 1830 to 1914:

(1) Extra margin on each page permits listing of library call numbers of often-used items.
(2) Extra space at the bottom of every page permits inclusion of additional entries.
(3) An index by author follows the bibliography proper.
(4) The index numbers direct the reader to the page and position-on-the-page of the desired entry. Thus, in an entry such as

Pritchard, J. P., 3.12,

the number 3.12 indicates that the entry referred to is on page 3, and is the 12th item on that page. Both page numbers and individual entry numbers are conspicuous in size and position so that the process of finding entries is fast as well as simple.

Symbols identifying journals follow the forms given in the List of Abbreviations at the beginning of the Bibliography. Items now available in paperback are followed by a dagger (†). An allusive title may be followed by a parenthetical indication of its topic.

Finally, the compiler would like to express his profound gratitude to his colleague, Professor G. Thomas Tanselle, for his expert assistance in standardizing the form of the entries in preparing the text for the typist. I am also very grateful to Mr. and Mrs. Charles Nelson for their help in verification and indexing.

A&W	Arizona and the West
AGAGC	Anglo-German and American-German Crosscurrents
AI	American Imago
AL	American Literature
ALR	American Literary Realism
Am Merc	American Mercury
Am R	American Review
APSR	American Political Science Review
AQ	American Quarterly
AR	Antioch Review
ArQ	Arizona Quarterly
AS	American Speech
ASEER	American Slavic and East European Review
ASch	American Scholar
AtlM	Atlantic Monthly
Aut.Aut	Milan Periodical

BAASB	British Association for American Studies Bulletin
BB	Bulletin of Bibliography
BFLS	Bulletin de la Faculté des Lettres de Strasbourg
BNYPL	Bulletin of the New York Public Library
BPLQ	Boston Public Library Quarterly
BRH	Bulletin des Recherches Historiques
BuR	Bucknell Review
BUSE	Boston University Studies in English
BuUS	Bucknell University Studies
BYUS	Brigham Young University Studies
CE	College English
CentM	Century Magazine
CHR	Canadian Historical Review
CL	Comparative Literature
CLAJ	College Language Association Journal
CLQ	Colby Library Quarterly
CLS	Comparative Literature Studies
CM	Cornhill Magazine
ColQ	Colorado Quarterly
CritQ	Critical Quarterly
CW	Classical Weekly
DA	Dissertation Abstracts
DD	Double Dealer
DN	Delaware Notes
DR	Dalhousie Review
EA	Etudes Anglaises
EIC	Essays in Criticism
EIHC	Essex Institute Historical Collections
EJ	English Journal
ELH	Journal of English Literary History
ELL	The English Language and Literature (Korea)
ER	Earlham Review
ESA	English Studies in Africa
ESQ	Emerson Society Quarterly
EUQ	Emory University Quarterly
Expl	Explicator
ForumH	Forum (Houston)
FurmS	Furman Studies
GaR	Georgia Review
GM	Gāndhi Mārg
GraM	Graham's Magazine
GRM	Germanisch-Romanische Monatsschrift
HarvR	Harvard Review
HGM	Harvard Graduate Magazine
HLB	Harvard Library Bulletin
HLQ	Huntington Library Quarterly
HomR	Homiletic Review
HR	Hispanic Review
HSNPL	Harvard Studies and Notes in Philology and Literature

HTR	Harvard Theological Review
HUB	Harvard University Bulletin
HudR	Hudson Review
HW	Harper's Weekly
IM	International Magazine
JA	Jahrbuch für Amerikastudien
JCMVASA	Journal of the Central Mississippi Valley American Studies Association
JEGP	Journal of English and Germanic Philology
JHAM	Johns Hopkins Alumni Magazine
JHI	Journal of the History of Ideas
JHR	Journal of Human Relations
JNH	Journal of Negro History
JNYES	Journal of the New York Entomological Society
JPE	Journal of Political Economy
JSH	Journal of Southern History
KAL	Kyushu American Literature
KR	Kenyon Review
L&P	Literature and Psychology
LanM	Les Langues Modernes
LH	Lincoln Herald
LHB	Lock Haven Bulletin
LHQ	Louisiana Historical Quarterly
LondM	London Mercury
LQ	Library Quarterly
LitRev	Little Review
MASJ	Midcontinent American Studies Journal
MF	Midwest Folklore
MFS	Modern Fiction Studies
MHSB	Missouri Historical Society Bulletin
MinnR	Minnesota Review
MissQ	Mississippi Quarterly
MJ	Midwest Journal
MLN	Modern Language Notes
MLQ	Modern Language Quarterly
MLR	Modern Language Review
ModA	Modern Age
ModQ	Modern Quarterly
MP	Modern Philology
MQ	Midwest Quarterly
MR	Massachusetts Review
MusQ	Musical Quarterly
MVHR	Mississippi Valley Historical Review
N&Q	Notes and Queries
NAR	North American Review
NCF	Nineteenth-Century Fiction
NCHR	North Carolina Historical Review
NCM	New-Church Messenger
NEQ	New England Quarterly

NewR	New Republic
NMQ	New Mexico Quarterly
NRS	Nuova Rivista Storica
NS	Die Neueren Sprachen
NY	New Yorker
NYH	New York History
OSAHQ	Ohio State Archaeological and Historical Quarterly
PAAAS	Proceedings of the American Academy of Arts and Sciences
PAAS	Proceedings of the American Antiquarian Society
PBSA	Papers of the Bibliographical Society of America
PCSM	Publications of the Colonial Society of Massachusetts
Person	The Personalist
PhilR	Philosophical Review
PHR	Pacific History Review
PMASAL	Papers of the Michigan Academy of Sciences, Arts, and Letters
PMHS	Proceedings of the Massachusetts Historical Society
PMLA	Publications of the Modern Language Association
PNJHS	Proceedings of the New Jersey Historical Society
Poetry R	Poetry Review
PQ	Philological Quarterly
PR	Partisan Review
PrS	Prairie Schooner
PSCS	Pennsylvania State College Studies
PSHA	Publications of the Southern Historical Association
PSQ	Political Science Quarterly
PUSA	Perspectives U.S.A.
QJS	Quarterly Journal of Speech
QNL	Quarterly News Letter (Book Club of California)
RAA	Revue Anglo-Américaine
RIP	Rice Institute Pamphlet
RJ	Romanistisches Jahrbuch
RLC	Revue de Littérature Comparée
RLMC	Rivista di Letterature Moderne e Comparate
RRel	Review of Religion
RS	Research Studies
S&S	Science and Society
SA	Studi Americani
SAQ	South Atlantic Quarterly
SatR	Saturday Review
SB	Studies in Bibliography
SCL	Studies in Comparative Literature
SCSH	Smith College Studies in History
SELit	Studies in English Literature (Tokyo)
SF	Social Forces
SFQ	Southern Folklore Quarterly
SIR	Studies in Romanticism
SL	Studia Linquistica (Lund, Sweden)
SLM	Southern Literary Messenger

SN	Studia Neophilologica
SoQ	Southern Quarterly
SoR	Southern Review
SP	Studies in Philology
SQ	Shakespeare Quarterly
SR	Sewanee Review
SRL	Saturday Review of Literature
SSF	Studies in Short Fiction
SUS	Susquehanna University Studies
SWR	Southwest Review
TCEL	Thought Currents in English Literature
TCL	Twentieth-Century Literature
TDK	Taisho Daigaku Kenkyukiyo
TexR	Texas Review
TexSE	Texas Studies in English
TSBooklet	Thoreau Society Booklet
TSE	Tulane Studies in English
TSL	Tennessee Studies in Literature
TSLL	Texas Studies in Literature and Language
TWA	Transactions of the Wisconsin Academy of Sciences, Arts and Letters
UCC	University of California Chronicle
UCPES	University of California Publications, English Studies
UCSLL	University of Colorado Studies in Language and Literature
UISLL	University of Illinois Studies in Language and Literature
UKCR	University of Kansas City Review
Umanesimo	Italian Quarterly of Italian and American Culture
UNCEB	University of North Carolina Extension Bulletin
UR	University Review
UTQ	University of Toronto Quarterly
UWP	University of Wyoming Publications
VMHB	Virginia Magazine of History and Biography
VQR	Virginia Quarterly Review
WAL	Western American Literature
WF	Western Folklore
WHR	Western Humanities Review
WMH	Wisconsin Magazine of History
WMQ	William and Mary Quarterly
WVUPP	West Virginia University Philological Papers
WWN	Walt Whitman Newsletter
WWR	Walt Whitman Review
XUS	Xavier University Studies
YCGL	Yearbook of Comparative and General Literature
YR	Yale Review
YULG	Yale University Library Gazette

NOTE: The publisher and compiler invite suggestions for additions to future editions of this bibliography.

Contents

I

Bibliographies and Reference Works

1 ADAMS, J. T., ed. *Dictionary of American History*. 5 vols. New York, 1940. (Sixth volume added 1961, ed. by J. G. E. Hopkins and Wayne Andrews.)

2 *American Quarterly*. (Beginning with 1967 this periodical carries an annual review of all books on American studies.)

3 BLANCK, Jacob, ed. *Bibliography of American Literature*. New Haven, 1955– . (In progress; five volumes so far published.)

4 GOHDES, Clarence. *Bibliographical Guide to the Study of the Literature of the U.S.A.* Durham, N.C., 1959. Rev. ed., 1964.

5 GOHDES, Clarence. *Literature and Theater of the States and Regions of the U.S.A.: An Historical Bibliography*. Durham, N.C., 1967.

6 HANDLIN, Oscar. *Harvard Guide to American History*. Cambridge, Mass., 1954.

7 HART, James D. *The Oxford Companion to American Literature*. 4th rev. ed. New York, 1965.

8 HERZBERG, Max, ed. *Reader's Encyclopedia of American Literature*. New York, 1962.

9 JOHNSON, Allen, and Dumas MALONE, eds. *Dictionary of American Biography*. 22 vols. New York, 1937.

10 JOHNSON, M. *Merle Johnson's American First Editions*. Rev. and enl. by Jacob Blanck. 4th ed. Waltham, Mass., 1965.

11 JOHNSON, Thomas H. *Literary History of the United States: Bibliography*. New York, 1948. *Bibliography Supplement*. Ed. by Richard M. Ludwig. New York, 1959.

12 JOHNSON, Thomas H. The Oxford Companion to American History. New York, 1966.

13 JONES, Howard M., and R. M. LUDWIG. *Guide to American Literature and its Background since 1890*. 3rd ed., rev. and enl. Cambridge, Mass., 1964.

14 KUNITZ, Stanley J., and Howard HAYCRAFT. *American Authors, 1600–1900*. New York, 1944.

15 KUNTZ, J. M. *Poetry Explication*. Denver, 1962.

16 LEARY, Lewis. *Articles on American Literature Appearing in Current Periodicals, 1900–1950*. Durham, N.C., 1954.

17 *MLA International Bibliography*. (Under various eds., published each May or June as an annual supplement to *PMLA*. Each issue lists articles and books of the preceding year.)

18 MOTT, F. L. *American Journalism: A History of Newspapers in the United States through 260 Years, 1690–1950*. Rev. ed. New York, 1959.

1 MOTT, F. L. *A History of American Magazines.* 5 vols. Cambridge, Mass., 1938–1968.
2 RUBIN, Louis, Jr. *A Bibliographical Guide to the Study of Southern Literature.* Baton Rouge, 1970.
3 STOVALL, Floyd, ed. *Eight American Authors. A Review of Research and Criticism.* New York, 1956. (Supplemented by J. C. Mathews in 1963 reprint.)†
4 TANSELLE, G. Thomas. "The Descriptive Bibliography of American Authors." *SB* 21(1968):1–24.
5 THRALL, W. F., Addison HIBBARD, and C. Hugh HOLMAN. *A Handbook to Literature.* Rev. ed. New York, 1960.
6 THURSTON, J. O., B. EMERSON, C. HARTMAN, and E. V. WRIGHT. *Short Fiction Criticism.* Denver, 1960.
7 TRENT, W. P., J. ERSKINE, S. P. SHERMAN, and Carl VAN DOREN, eds. *Cambridge History of American Literature.* 4 vols. New York, 1917–1921. (Bibliographies for each chapter.)
8 TURNER, Darwin T., comp. *Afro-American Writers.* New York, 1970.
9 WOODRESS, James. *Dissertations in American Literature, 1891–1966.* Rev. ed. Durham, N.C., 1968.
10 WOODRESS, James, ed. *American Literary Scholarship: An Annual.* Durham, N.C., 1963– . (Covers 1963 to the present.)

Backgrounds

11 BEARD, Charles and Mary. *The Rise of American Civilization.* 4 vols. New York, 1927–1942.
12 CURTI, Merle. *The Growth of American Thought.* New York, 1943. 3d rev. ed. 1964.
13 DORFMAN, Joseph. *The Economic Mind in American Civilization.* 5 vols. New York, 1946–1959.
14 GABRIEL, Ralph H. *The Course of American Democratic Thought.* New York, 1940.
15 HARTMANN, S. *A History of American Art.* 2 vols. Boston, 1902; rev., 1934.
16 HOFSTADTER, Richard. *Social Darwinism in American Thought, 1860–1915.* Rev. ed. New York, 1959.†
17 JENSEN, Merrill, ed. *Regionalism in America.* Madison, Wis., 1951.
18 LARKIN, O. W. *Art and Life in America.* New York, 1949.
19 NEVINS, Allan et al., eds. *Civil War Books: A Critical Bibliography.* 2 vols. Baton Rouge, 1967–1968. (5700 entries, critically appraised.)
20 PERSONS, Stow, ed. *Impact of Evolution on American Thought.* New Haven, 1950.

1 SCHLESINGER, Arthur, and D. R. FOX, general eds. *A History of American Life*. 13 vols. New York, 1927–1931. (See C. R. Fish, *The Rise of the Common Man*; A. H. Cole, *The Irrepressible Conflict*; Allan Nevins, *The Emergence of Modern America, 1865–1878*; A. M. Schlesinger, *The Rise of the City*; Faulkner, *The Quest of Social Justice*.)

2 SCHNEIDER, H. W. *A History of American Philosophy*. New York, 1946.

3 STEPHENSON, W. H., and E. M. COULTER, eds. *A History of the South*. 10 vols. Baton Rouge, 1951ff. (Includes L. Van Woodward, *The Origins of the New South, 1877–1913*.)

4 SWEET, W. W. *Religion in the Development of American Culture, 1765–1840*. New York, 1952. (See also files of the periodical *Church History*.)

5 TOWNSEND, H. G. *Philosophical Ideas in the United States*. New York, 1934.

6 TURNER, F. J. *The Frontier in American History*. New York, 1920.

7 TURNER, F. J. *The Significance of Sections in American History*. New York, 1932.

8 WECTER, Dixon. *The Saga of American Society, 1607–1937*. New York, 1937.

9 WISH, Harvey. *Society and Thought in America*. 2 vols. New York, 1950–1952.

Literary History

10 ABBOT, M., ed. *American Renaissance, the History and Literature of an Era: Essays and Interpretations*. Frankfurt, 1961.

11 *American Writers' Series*. General ed., Harry H. Clark. New York, 1934–1950. (Twenty-four volumes with long introductions and annotated bibliographies.)

12 ASSELINEAU, Roger. "The French Stream in American Literature," *YCGL* 17(1968):29–39.

13 BERTHOFF, Warner. *The Ferment of Realism in American Literature, 1884–1919*. New York, 1965.

14 BEWLEY, M. *The Complex Fate*. London, 1952.

15 BIER, Jesse. *The Rise and Fall of American Humor*. New York, 1968.

16 BLAIR, Walter. *Horse Sense in American Humor*. Chicago, 1942.

17 BLAIR, Walter. *Native American Humor*. New York, 1937.†

18 BOAS, G. *Romanticism in America*. Baltimore, 1940.

19 BODE, Carl. *The American Lyceum*. New York, 1956.

1   BODE, Carl, ed. *The Young Rebel in American Literature.* New York, 1960.

2   BOGAN, Louise. *Achievement in American Poetry, 1900–1950.* Chicago, 1951.†

3   BOWERS, D. F., ed. *Foreign Influences in American Life: Essays and Critical Bibliographies.* Princeton, 1944.†

4   BRANCH, E. D. *The Cowboy and His Interpreters.* New York, 1961.

5   BROOKS, Van Wyck. *Makers and Finders: A History of the Writer in America, 1800–1915.* 5 vols. New York, 1952.

6   BROWN, C. A., comp. *The Achievement of American Criticism.* New York, 1954. (Bibliographies, pp. 688–724.)

7   BROWN, H. R. *The Sentimental Novel in America, 1789–1860.* Durham, North Carolina, 1940.

8   CADY, Edwin H. *The Gentleman in America.* Syracuse, 1949.

9   CARGILL, Oscar. *Intellectual America: Ideas on the March.* New York, 1941. (From about 1870.)

10   CAWELTI, J. G. *Apostles of the Self-Made Man.* Chicago, 1965.†

11   CHARVAT, William. *The Profession of Authorship in America.* Columbus, 1968.

12   CLARK, Harry H. "The Influence of Science on American Literary Criticism, 1860–1910, Including the Vogue of Taine." *TWA* 44(1955):109–164.

13   CLARK, Harry H., ed. *Transitions in American Literary History.* Durham, N.C., 1954.

14   COMMAGER, Henry Steele. *The American Mind.* New Haven, 1950.

15   CONNER, F. W. *Cosmic Optimism: A Study of the Interpretation of Evolution by American Poets from Emerson to Robinson.* Gainesville, Fla., 1949.

16   COWIE, Alexander. *The Rise of the American Novel.* New York, 1948.

17   CURTI, Merle E. *Human Nature in American Historical Thought.* Columbia, Mo., 1968.

18   DENNEY, M., and W. H. GILMAN, eds. *The American Writer and the European Tradition.* New York, 1964.

19   DORFMAN, Joseph. *The Economic Mind in American Civilization.* 5 vols. New York, 1946–1959.

20   EARNEST, Ernest. *Expatriots and Patriots: American Artists, Scholars and Writers in Europe.* Durham, N.C., 1968.

21   EKIRCH, A. A., Jr. *The Idea of Progress in America, 1815–1860.* New York, 1951.

22   FEIDELSON, Charles, Jr. *Symbolism and American Literature.* Chicago, 1953.†

23   FIEDLER, Leslie A. *Love and Death in the American Novel.* New York, 1960, rev. 1966.†

24   FISCHEL, Leslie, Jr., and Benjamin QUARLES, eds. *The Negro American: A Documentary History.* New York, 1968.

1 FLOAN, H. R. *The South in Northern Eyes, 1831–1861.* Austin, 1958.
2 FLORY, C. R. *Economic Criticism in American Fiction, 1792–1900.* Philadelphia, 1936.
3 FOERSTER, Norman. *American Criticism.* Boston, 1928.
4 FOERSTER, Norman. *Nature in American Literature.* New York, 1923.
5 FRENCH, Warren. *The Social Novel at the End of an Era.* Carbondale, Ill., 1966.
6 FUSSELL, E. S. *The Frontier: American Literature and the American West.* Princeton, 1965.
7 GARDINER, H. C., ed. *American Classics Reconsidered: A Christian [Catholic] Appraisal.* New York, 1958.
8 GEISMAR, Maxwell D. *The Last of the Provincials.* Boston, 1947.†
9 GELFANT, B. H. *The American City Novel.* Norman, Okla., 1954.
10 GODDARD, H. C. *Studies in New England Transcendentalism.* New York, 1908, 1960.
11 GOHDES, Clarence. *American Literature in Nineteenth Century England.* New York, 1944.†
12 GOHDES, Clarence. *The Periodicals of American Transcendentalism.* Durham, N.C., 1931.
13 GREGORY, Horace, and M. ZATURENSKA. *A History of American Poetry, 1900–1940.* New York, 1946.
14 GUTTMAN, Allan. *The Conservative Tradition in America.* New York, 1967.
15 HALL, Wade. *The Smiling Phoenix: A Study of Southern Humor, 1865–1914.* Gainesville, Fla., 1965.
16 HARTMANN, S. *A History of American Art.* 2 vols. Boston, 1902; rev., 1934.
17 HARTWICK, Harry. *Foreground of American Fiction.* New York, 1934. (Includes short stories.)
18 HAZARD, L. L. *The Frontier in American Literature.* New York, 1927.
19 HOFFMAN, Daniel G. *Form and Fable in American Fiction.* New York, 1961.†
20 HOWARD, Leon. *Literature and the American Tradition.* Garden City, New York, 1960.†
21 HUBBELL, Jay B. *The South in American Literature, 1607–1900.* Durham, N.C., 1954.
22 JONES, Howard M. *American and French Culture.* Chapel Hill, N.C. 1927.
23 JONES, Howard M. *Guide to American Literature and Its Backgrounds since 1890.* 3rd ed. Cambridge, Mass., 1964.
24 JONES, Howard M. *A Strange New World: American Culture: The Formative Years.* New York, 1964.
25 JONES, Howard M. *The Theory of American Literature.* Reissued with a New Concluding Chapter and Revised Bibliography. Ithaca, N.Y., 1965.

1   KAUL, A. N. *The American Vision.* New Haven, 1963.

2   KAZIN, Alfred. *On Native Grounds: An Interpretation of Modern American Prose Literature.* New York, 1942.†

3   KNIGHT, G. C. *The Critical Period in American Literature, 1890–1900.* Chapel Hill, N.C., 1951.

4   KNIGHT, G. C. *The Strenuous Age in American Literature, 1900–1910.* Chapel Hill, N.C., 1954.

5   KOLB, Harold H., Jr. *The Illusion of Life: American Realism as a Literary Form.* Charlottesville, Va., 1969.

6   KRAUS, Michael. *A History of American History.* New York, 1937.

7   KREYMBORG, Alfred. *A History of American Poetry, 1620–1930.* New York, 1934. (A reissue of *Our Singing Strength,* 1929.)

8   KWIAT, J. J., and M. C. TURPIE, eds. *Studies in American Culture: Dominant Ideas and Images.* Minneapolis, 1960.

9   LASCH, Christopher. *The New Radicalism in America: The Intellectual as a Social Type, 1889–1963.* New York, 1965.†

10   LEISY, E. E. *The American Historical Novel.* Norman, Okla., 1950.

11   LEWIS, R. W. B. *The American Adam: Innocence, Tragedy, and Tradition in the Nineteenth Century.* Chicago, 1955, 1959, 1964.†

12   LOGGINS, V. *The Negro Author: His Development in America to 1900.* Port Washington, N.Y., 1964.

13   LONG, O. W. *Literary Pioneers.* Cambridge, Mass., 1936.

14   McMAHON, H. *Criticism of Fiction: A Study of Trends in the Atlantic Monthly, 1857–1898.* New York, 1952.

15   MACY, J. A., ed. *American Writers on American Literature.* New York, 1931.

16   MARTIN, Jay. *Harvests of Change: American Literature, 1865–1914.* Englewood Cliffs, N.J., 1967.

17   MARX, L. *The Machine in the Garden: Technology and the Pastoral Ideal in America.* New York, 1964.†

18   MATTHIESSEN, F. O. *American Renaissance: Art and Expression in the Age of Emerson and Whitman.* London, 1941.†

19   MENCKEN, H. L. *The American Language: An Inquiry into the Development of English in the United States.* New York, 1936. *Supplement I,* 1945; *II,* 1948.

20   MERRILL, D. K. *The Development of American Biography.* Portland, Me., 1932.

21   MILLER, James E., Jr. *Quests Surd and Absurd: Essays in American Literature.* Chicago, 1967.

22   MILLER, Perry. *Nature's Nation.* Cambridge, Mass., 1967.

23   MILLER, Perry, ed. *The Transcendentalists: An Anthology.* Cambridge, Mass., 1950.

24   MORGAN, H. Wayne. *American Writers in Rebellion: From Mark Twain to Dreiser.* New York, 1965.

25   MIZENER, Arthur. *Twelve Great American Novels.* New York, 1967.

LITERARY HISTORY 7

1 MOTT, F. L. *Golden Multitudes: The Story of Best Sellers in the United States.* New York, 1947.
2 O'CONNOR, W. V. *The Age of Criticism, 1900–1950.* Chicago, 1952.†
3 O'CONNOR, W. V. *Sense and Sensibility in American Poetry.* Chicago, 1948.
4 O'NEILL, Edward H. *Biography by Americans, 1658–1936: A Subject Bibliography.* Philadelphia, 1939.
5 OSTERWEIS, Rollin G. *Romanticism and Nationalism in the Old South.* Athens, Ga., 1963.†
6 PARKS, Edd W. *Antebellum Literary Criticism in the South.* Athens, Ga., 1963.
7 PARRINGTON, V. L. *Main Currents in American Thought: An Interpretation of American Literature from the Beginnings to 1920.* 3 vols. New York, 1927–1930.†
8 PATTEE, F. L. *The Development of the American Short Story.* New York, 1923.
9 PATTEE, F. L. *A History of American Literature since 1870.* New York, 1915.
10 PEARCE, R. H. *The Continuity of American Poetry.* Princeton, 1961.†
11 PIZER, Donald. *Realism and Naturalism in Nineteenth Century American Literature.* Carbondale, Ill., 1966.
12 POCHMANN, H. A. *German Culture in America.* Madison, 1956.
13 POIRIER, Richard. *A World Elsewhere: The Place of Style in American Literature.* New York, 1966.†
14 PORTE, Joel. *The Romance in America: Studies in Cooper, Poe, Hawthorne, Melville, and James.* Middletown, 1969.
15 PRITCHARD, John P. *Criticism in America.* Norman, Okla., 1956.
16 PRITCHARD, John P. *Literary Wise Men of Gotham: Criticism in New York, 1815–1860.* Baton Rouge, La., 1963.
17 QUINN, Arthur H. *American Fiction: An Historical and Critical Survey.* New York, 1936.
18 QUINN, Arthur H., ed. *Literature of the American People.* New York, 1951.
19 RAHV, Philip, ed. *Discovery of Europe.* With Introduction. Garden City, New York, 1960. (Paperback reissue of 1947 anthology from Franklin through William James.)
20 REGIER, C. C. *The Era of the Muckrakers.* Chapel Hill, North Carolina, 1932.
21 ROSE, L. A. "A Bibliographical Survey of Economic and Political [Belletristic] Writings, 1865–1900." *AL*, 15(1944):381–410. Supplements I and II in mimeographed form, April and October, 1944, Houghton, Mich.
22 ROURKE, Constance. *American Humor: A Study of the National Character.* New York, 1931.†

1   RUSK, R. L. *The Literature of the Middle Western Frontier.* 2 vols. New York, 1925.

2   SANFORD, C. *The Quest for Paradise: Europe and American Moral Imagination.* Urbana, Ill., 1961.

3   SCHNEIDER, H. W. *A History of American Philosophy.* New York, 1946.†

4   SIMON, Myron, and Thornton H. PARSONS, eds. *Transcendentalism and Its Legacy.* Ann Arbor, 1966.

5   SKARD, Sigmund, ed. *Americana Norvegica: Norwegian Contributions to American Studies.* Vol. I. Philadelphia, 1966.

6   SKARD, Sigmund, and H. H. WASSER, eds. *Americana Norvegica: Novegian Contributions to American Studies.* Vol. II. Philadelphia, 1970.

7   SMITH, Henry N. *Virgin Land: The American West as Symbol and Myth.* Cambridge, Mass., 1950.†

8   SPENCER, B. *The Quest for Nationality.* Syracuse, N.Y., 1957.

9   SPILLER, Robert E.; Willard Thorp; Thomas H. Johnson; and Henry S. Canby, eds. *Literary History of the United States.* 3 vols. New York, 1949. 2nd rev. ed., New York, 1963.

10 STOVALL, Floyd, ed. *The Development of American Literary Criticism: A Symposium.* Chapel Hill, N.C., 1955.†

11 STOVALL, Floyd, ed. *Eight American Authors: A Review of Research and Criticism.* New York, 1956. Supplemented by J. C. Mathews in 1963 repr.†

12 STRAUCH, Carl F., ed. "Critical Symposium on American Romanticism." *ESQ*, 35(1964):2–60.

13 STROUT, C. *The American Image of the Old World.* New York, 1963.

14 TAYLOR, W. F. *The Economic Novel in America.* Chapel Hill, N.C., 1942.

15 VAN DOREN, Carl. *The American Novel.* New York, 1940.

16 WAGENKNECHT, Edward. *Cavalcade of the American Novel.* New York, 1954.

17 WAGGONER, H. H. *American Poets.* Boston, 1968.

18 WAGGONER, H. H. *The Heel of Elohim: Science and Values in Modern American Poetry.* Norman, Okla., 1950.

19 WALCUTT, C. C. *American Literary Naturalism: A Divided Stream.* Minneapolis, 1956.

20 WELLS, H. W. *The American Way of Poetry.* New York, 1943.

21 WEST, R. B. *The Short Story in America, 1900–1950.* Chicago, 1952.

22 WESTBROOK, G. L. *Acres of Flint: Writers of Rural New England, 1870–1900.* Washington, 1951.

23 WILLIAMS, S. T. *The Beginnings of American Poetry, 1620–1855.* Uppsala, Sweden, 1951.

1 WILLIAMS, S. T. *The Spanish Background of American Literature.* 2 vols. New Haven, 1955.
2 WILSON, Edmund. *Patriotic Gore: Studies in the Literature of the American Civil War.* New York, 1962.†
3 WISH, H. *The American Historian: A Social-Intellectual History of the Writing of the American Past.* New York, 1960.†
4 ZIFF, Larzer. *The American 1890's: The Life and Times of a Lost Generation.* New York, 1966.†

Major American Writers

Henry Adams (*1838–1918*)

Texts

5 *Chapters of Erie and Other Essays.* In collaboration with Charles F. Adams, Jr. Boston, 1871.†
6 *The Life of Albert Gallatin.* Philadelphia, 1879.
7 *Democracy: An American Novel.* New York, 1880.†
8 *John Randolph.* Boston, 1882.
9 *Esther: A Novel.* New York, 1884.
10 *History of the United States of America during the Administrations of Thomas Jefferson and James Madison.* 9 vols. New York, 1889–1891.†
11 *Historical Essays.* New York, 1891.
12 *Memoirs of Marau Taaroa, Last Queen of Tahiti.* Trans. and ed. by Henry Adams. Privately printed, 1893. Repub., rev. and enl. as *Memoirs of Arii Taimai E.* Paris, 1901.
13 *Mont-Saint-Michel and Chartres.* Washington, 1904.†
14 *The Education of Henry Adams.* Washington, 1907. (Numerous editions.)†
15 *The Life of George Cabot Lodge.* Boston, 1911.
16 "Buddha and Brahma." *YR*, 5(1915):82–89.
17 *The Degradation of the Democratic Dogma.* Ed. by Brooks Adams. New York, 1919. (Contains "Tendency of History," *The Rule of Phase Applied to History*, and *A Letter to American Teachers of History*.)
18 *Letters to a Niece and Prayer to the Virgin of Chartres, with a Niece's Memories.* Ed. by Mabel La Farge. Boston, 1920.
19 *A Cycle of Adams Letters 1861–1965.* Ed. by Worthington C. Ford. 2 vols. Boston, 1930.
20 *Letters of Henry Adams 1858–1918.* Ed. by Worthington C. Ford 2 vols. Boston, 1930–1938.

1   *Henry Adams and His Friends.* Ed. by Harold Dean Cater. Boston, 1947.
2   *The Great Secession Winter of 1860–61 and Other Essays.* Ed. by George Hochfield. New York, 1958. (Contains fourteen essays.)†

Biographies

3   ADAMS, James Truslow. *Henry Adams.* New York, 1933.
4   SAMUELS, Ernest. *The Young Henry Adams; Henry Adams: The Middle Years; Henry Adams: The Major Phase.* Cambridge, Mass., 1948, 1958, 1964.
5   STEVENSON, Elizabeth. *Henry Adams: A Biography.* New York, 1956.†

Critical Studies

6   BAYM, Max I. *The French Education of Henry Adams.* New York, 1951.
7   BAYM, Max I. "William James and Henry Adams." *NEQ,* 10(1937):717–742.
8   BECKER, Carl L. *Every Man His Own Historian.* New York, 1935.†
9   BLACKMUR, Richard P. "The Atlantic Unites." *HudR,* 5(1952):212–232.
10   BLACKMUR, Richard P. "The Expense of Greatness." *VQR* 11(1936):396–415.
11   BLACKMUR, Richard P. "The Harmony of True Liberalism: Henry Adams' *Mont-Saint-Michel and Chartres.*" *SR,* 60(1952):1–27.
12   BONNER, Thomas N. "Henry Adams: A Sketch and an Analysis." *Historian,* 20(1957):58–79.
13   BRADFORD, Gamaliel. *American Portraits, 1875–1900.* Boston, 1922.
14   BROOKS, Van Wyck. *New England: Indian Summer, 1865–1915.* New York, 1940.†
15   CAIRNS, John C. "The Successful Quest of Henry Adams." *SAQ,* 57(1958):168–193.
16   COLACURCIO, Michael. "The Dynamo and the Angelic Doctor: The Bias of Henry Adams' Medievalism." *AQ,* 17(1965):696–712.
17   COMMAGER, Henry Steele. "Henry Adams." In *The Marcus W. Jernegan Essays in American Historiography.* Ed. by William T. Hutchinson. Chicago, 1937.
18   CONDER, John. *A Formula of his Own: Henry Adams' Literary Experiment.* Chicago, 1970.
19   FOLSOM, James K. "Mutation as Metaphor in *The Education of Henry Adams.*" *ELH,* 30(1963):162–174.
20   GABRIEL, Ralph H. *The Course of American Democratic Thought.* New York, 1940.

1 GLICKSBERG, Charles I. "Henry Adams and the Aesthetic Quest." *PrS*, 25(1951):241–250.

2 HOCHFIELD, George. *Henry Adams.* New York, 1962.†

3 HOFSTADTER, Richard. *Social Darwinism in American Thought, 1860–1915.* Philadelphia, 1945.†

4 HOWE, Irving. *Politics and the Novel.* New York, 1957.†

5 HUME, Robert A. *Runaway Star: An Appreciation of Henry Adams.* Ithaca, N.Y., 1951.

6 HUME, Robert A. "The Style and Literary Background of Henry Adams." *AL*, 16(1945):296–315.

7 JORDY, William. "Henry Adams and Francis Parkman." *AQ*, 3(1951): 52–68.

8 JORDY, William. *Henry Adams: Scientific Historian.* New Haven, 1952.

9 KARIEL, Henry S. "The Limits of Social Science: Henry Adams' Quest for Order." *APSR*, 50(1956):1074–1092.

10 LEVENSON, J. C. *The Mind and Art of Henry Adams.* Boston, 1957.†

11 LYON, Melvin. *Symbol and Idea in Henry Adams.* Lincoln, Neb., 1970.

12 MacLEAN, Kenneth. "Window and Cross in Henry Adams' *Education*." *UTQ*, 28(1959):332–344.

13 MAUD, Ralph. "Henry Adams: Irony and Impasse." *EIC*, 8(1958): 381–392.

14 MENDEL, Joseph. "The Use of Metaphor: Henry Adams and the Symbols of Science." *JHI*, 26(1955):89–102.

15 MORE, Paul E. *A New England Group and Others.* (*Shelburne Essays*, Eleventh Series.) Boston, 1921.

16 MUNFORD, Howard M. "Henry Adams and the Tendency of History." *NEQ*, 32(1959):79–90.

17 NICHOLS, Roy. "The Dynamic Interpretation of History." *NEQ*, 8(1935):163–178.

18 NUHN, Ferner. *The Wind Blew From the East.* New York, 1942.

19 PARRINGTON, Vernon Louis. *Main Currents in American Thought*, Vol. 3. New York, 1930.†

20 PERSONS, Stow, ed. *Evolutionary Thought in America.* New Haven, 1950.

21 PETERSON, Merrill D. "Henry Adams on Jefferson the President." *VQR*, 39(1963):187–201. (See also his *The Jeffersonian Image in the American Mind.* New York, 1963.)

22 RULAND, Richard. "Tocqueville's *de la Démocratie en Amerique* and *The Education of Henry Adams*." *CLS*, 2(1965):195–207.

23 SABINE, G. H. "Henry Adams and the Writing of History." *UCC*, 26(1924):31–46.

24 SAVETH, Edward N. "The Heroines of Henry Adams." *AQ* 8(1956): 231–242.

12 MAJOR AMERICAN WRITERS

1 SAYRE, Robert F. *The Examined Self: Benjamin Franklin, Henry Adams, and Henry James.* Princeton, 1964. (A study of autobiographies.)

2 SCHEYER, Ernst. "The Aesthete Henry Adams." *Criticism*, 4(1962): 313–327.

3 SHAW, Peter. "Blood is Thicker than Irony: Henry Adams' *History.*" *NEQ*, 40(1967):163–187.

4 SPEARE, Morris Edmund. *The Political Novel.* New York, 1924.

5 SPILLER, Robert E. "Henry Adams." In *Literary History of the United States*, Vol. 2. New York, 1949.

6 SAMUELS, Ernest. "Henry Adams." In *Major Writers of America.* Ed. by Perry Miller. New York, 1962.

7 WAGNER, Vern. "The Lotus of Henry Adams." *NEQ*, 27(1954):75–95.

8 WAGNER, Vern. *The Suspension of Henry Adams: A Study in Manner and Matter.* Detroit, 1969.

9 WASSER, Henry. *The Scientific Thought of Henry Adams.* Thessaloniki, 1956.

10 WASSER, Henry. "The Thought of Henry Adams." *NEQ*, 24(1951): 495–509.

11 WHIPPLE, T. K. *Spokesmen, Modern Writers and American Life.* New York, 1928.

12 WHITE, Lynn, Jr. "Dynamo and Virgin Reconsidered." *ASch*, 27(1958): 183–194.

13 WINKS. Robin W. "Henry Adams' Philosophy of History." *DR*, 44(1964): 199–204.

14 WINTERS, Yvor. *In Defense of Reason.* New York, 1947.†

15 WISH, Harvey. *The American Historian.* New York, 1960.†

16 WRIGHT, Nathalia. "Henry Adams's Theory of History: A Puritan Defense." *NEQ*, 17(1945):204–210.

Samuel L. Clemens ["Mark Twain"] (1835–1910)

Bibliographies

17 BEEBE, Maurice, and FEASTER, John. "Criticism of Mark Twain: A Selected Checklist." *Modern Fiction Studies*, 14(1968):93–139.

18 CLARK, Harry H. "Mark Twain." In *Eight American Authors.* Ed. by F. Stovall. New York, 1956. (Supplemented by J. C. Mathews in 1963 printing.)

19 JOHNSON, Merle. *A Bibliography of the Works of Mark Twain.* Rev. ed. New York, 1935.

Texts

1 *The Writings of Mark Twain.* Ed. by Albert B. Paine. 37 vols. New York, 1922–1925. (This is standard for what it contains, but it will be superseded by a new collected edition being issued under the editorship of John Gerber. Frederick Anderson is editing *Mark Twain's Papers*, unfinished or of a business concern.)

2 *Mark Twain's Western Years.* Ed. by Ivan Benson. Stanford, Calif., 1938. (With long introductory chapters.)

3 *Mark Twain in Eruption.* Ed. by Bernard DeVoto. New York, 1940.†

4 *The Letters of Quintus Curtius Snodgrass.* Ed. by E. E. Leisy. Dallas, 1946. (Allan Bates, *AL*, 36(1964):31–37 questions Twain's authorship of the Snodgrass Letters.)

5 *Love Letters of Mark Twain.* Ed. by Dixon Wecter. New York, 1949.

6 *Mark Twain of the "Enterprise."* Ed. by Henry N. Smith. Berkeley, Calif., 1957.

7 *The Autobiography of Mark Twain, Including Chapters Now Published for the First Time.* Ed. with an Introduction by Charles Neider. New York, 1959.†

8 *Mark Twain-Howells Letters.* 2 vols. Ed. by W. M. Gibson and H. N. Smith. Cambridge, Mass., 1960 (with notes).

9 *Life As I Find It: Essays, Sketches, Tales and Other Material, the Majority of Which Is Now Published in Book Form for the First Time.* Introduction and Notes by Charles Neider. Garden City, N.Y., 1961.

10 *The Art of Huckleberry Finn: Text, Sources, Criticisms.* Ed. by Hamlin Hill, and Walter Blair. San Francisco, 1962. (Facsimile of first edition with sources and critical essays by various hands.)†

11 *Letters from the Earth.* Ed. by Bernard De Voto. Introduction by Henry Nash Smith. New York, 1962. (Previously unpublished writings.)†

12 *Mark Twain's Letters to His Publishers, 1867–1894.* Ed. with an introduction by Hamlin Hill. Berkeley, Calif., 1967.

13 *Mark Twain's Satires and Burlesques.* Ed. with an Introduction by Franklin R. Rogers. Berkeley, Calif., 1968.

14 *Mark Twain's "Which Was the Dream?" and Other Symbolic Writings of the Later Years.* Ed. with an Introduction by John S. Tuckey. Berkeley, Calif., 1968.

15 *Mark Twain's Correspondence with Henry Huttleston Rogers 1893–1909.* Ed. by Lewis Leary. Berkeley, 1969.

16 *Mark Twain's Hannibal, Huck and Tom.* Ed. by Walter Blair. Berkeley, 1969.

17 *Mark Twain's Mysterious Stranger Manuscripts.* Ed. by William Gibson. Berkeley, 1969.

Biographies

18 DeVOTO, Bernard. *Mark Twain's America.* Boston, 1932.

1 FERGUSON, DeLANCEY. *Mark Twain: Man and Legend.* Ind., 1943.†
2 HENDERSON, Archibald. *Mark Twain.* London, 1911.
3 KAPLAN, Justin. *Mr. Clemens and Mark Twain: A Biography.* New York, 1966.†
4 MASTERS, Edgar Lee. *Mark Twain: A Portrait.* New York, 1938.
5 PAINE, Albert B. *Mark Twain: A Biography.* 3 vols. New York, 1912.
6 TURNER, Arlin. *Mark Twain and George W. Cable.* East Lansing, Mich., 1960.
7 WECTER, Dixon. *Sam Clemens of Hannibal.* Ed. by Elizabeth Wecter. Boston, 1952. (Clemens' childhood and adolescence.)†

Critical Studies

8 ALLEN, Jerry. *The Adventures of Mark Twain.* Boston, 1954.†
9 ANDREWS, Kenneth R. *Nook Farm: Mark Twain's Hartford Circle.* Cambridge, Mass., 1950.
10 BAETZHOLD, Howard G. "The Course of Composition of *A Connecticut Yankee:* A Reinterpretation." *AL,* 33(1961):195–214.
11 BAETZHOLD, Howard G. *Mark Twain and John Bull: The British Connection.* Bloomington, Ind., 1970.
12 BAETZHOLD, Howard G. "Mark Twain: England's Advocate." *AL,* 30(1956):328–346.
13 BALDANZA, Frank. *Mark Twain: An Introduction and Interpretation.* New York, 1961.†
14 BELLAMY, Gladys Carmen. *Mark Twain as a Literary Artist.* Norman, Okla., 1950. (One of two best works of literary criticism.)
15 BENARDETE, Jane J. "*Huckleberry Finn* and the Nature of Fiction." *MR,* 9(1968):209–226.
16 BLAIR, Walter. "The French Revolution and *Huckleberry Finn.*" *MP,* 55(1957):21–35.
17 BLAIR, Walter. *Mark Twain & Huck Finn.* Berkeley, Calif., 1960. (Best single critical-historical study of *Huck Finn.*)†
18 BLAIR, Walter. "When was *Huckleberry Finn* Written?" *AL,* 30(1958):1–25.
19 BLUES, Thomas. *Mark Twain and the Community.* Lexington, Ky., 1970.
20 BRADLEY, Sculley, R. C. BEATTY, and E. H. LONG, eds. *Adventures of Huckleberry Finn: An Annotated Text, Backgrounds, and Sources. Essays in Criticism.* New York, 1962. (Criticism by various hands.)†
21 BRANCH, Edgar Marquess. *The Literary Apprenticeship of Mark Twain.* Urbana, Ill., 1950.
22 BRANCH, Edgar Marquess, ed. *Clemens of the Call: Mark Twain in San Francisco.* Berkeley, 1970.
23 BRASHEAR, Minnie M. *Mark Twain, Son of Missouri.* Chapel Hill, N.C., 1934.
24 BROOKS, Van Wyck. *The Ordeal of Mark Twain.* Rev. ed. New York, 1933. (Most provocative of Mark Twain studies.)
25 BUDD, Louis J. "Mark Twain Plays the Bachelor." *WHR,* 11(1957):157–167.

1 BUDD, Louis J. *Mark Twain: Social Philosopher*. Bloomington, Ind., 1962.†

2 BUDD, Louis J. "The Southward Currents Under Huck Finn's Raft." *MVHR*, 66(1959):222–237.

3 BUDD, Louis J. "Twain, Howells, and the Boston Nihilists." *NEQ*, 32(1959):351–371.

4 CANBY, Henry Seidel. *Turn West, Turn East*. Boston, 1951. (A biographical comparison with Henry James.)

5 CARDWELL, Guy A. *Twins of Genius: Letters of Mark Twain, George W. Cable and Others*. East Lansing, Mich., 1953.

6 CARTER, P. J., Jr. "The Influence of the Nevada Frontier on Mark Twain." *WHR*, 13(1959):61–70.

7 CARTER, P. J., Jr. "Mark Twain and the American Labor Movement." *NEQ*, 30(1957):382–388.

8 CARTER, P. J., Jr. "Mark Twain: 'Moralist in Disguise'." *UCSLL*, 6(1957):65–79.

9 COVICI, Pascal, Jr. *Mark Twain's Humor: The Image of a World*. Dallas, Tex., 1962.

10 COX, J. M. "*A Connecticut Yankee in King Arthur's Court:* The Machinery of Self-Preservation." *YR*, 50(1960):89–102.

11 COX, J. M. "*Pudd'nhead Wilson:* The End of Mark Twain's American Dream." *SAQ* 58(1959):351–363.

12 CUMMINGS, S. "Mark Twain and the Sirens of Progress." *JCMVASA*, 1(1960):17–24.

13 CUMMINGS, S. "Mark Twain's Social Darwinism." *HLQ*, 20(1957): 163–175.

14 CUMMINGS, S. "Science and Mark Twain's Theory of Fiction." *PQ*, 37(1958):26–33.

15 DARBEE, H., ed. "Mark Twain in Hartford: The Happy Years." *AH*, 10(Dec. 1959):65–80.

16 DE VOTO, Bernard. *Mark Twain at Work*. Cambridge, Mass., 1942.†

17 DE VOTO, Bernard. *Mark Twain's America*. Boston, 1932. (Spirited reply to Brooks.)†

18 DUROCHER, A. A. "Mark Twain and the Roman Catholic Church." *JCMVASA*, 1(1960):32–43.

19 DYSON, A. E. "Huckleberry Finn and the Whole Truth." *CritQ*, 3(Spring 1961):29–40.

20 ELIOT, T. S. "Introduction" to *The Adventures of Huckleberry Finn*. London, 1950.

21 FATOUT, Paul. *Mark Twain in Virginia City*. Bloomington, Ind., 1964.

22 FATOUT, Paul. *Mark Twain on the Lecture Circuit*. Bloomington, Ind., 1960.

23 FONER, Philip S. *Mark Twain: Social Critic*. New York, 1958.†

1   FRANTZ, R. W., Jr. "The Role of Folklore in *Huckleberry Finn*." *AL* 28(1956):314–327.

2   GANZEL, D. "Twain, Travel Books, and *Life on the Mississippi*." *AL*, 34(1962):40–55.

3   GERBER, J. C. "Mark Twain's Use of the Comic Pose." *PMLA*, 77(1962): 297–304.

4   GERBER, J. C. "The Relations between Point of View and Style in the Works of Mark Twain." In *Style in Prose Fiction: English Institute Essays.* Ed. by H. C. Martin. New York, 1959.

5   GIBSON, William M. "Mark Twain's *Mysterious Stranger* Manuscripts: Some Questions for Textual Critics." *Bulletin of the Rocky Mountain Modern Language Association.* (1968):183–191.

6   HILL, H. L. "The Composition and the Structure of *Tom Sawyer*." *AL*, 32(1961):379–392.

7   HILL, H. L. "Mark Twain's Book Sales, 1869–1879." *BNYPL*, 65(1961): 371–389.

8   HILL, H. L. "Mark Twain's 'Brace of Brief Lectures on Science'." *NEQ*, 34(1961):228–239.

9   HILL, H. L. "Mark Twain's Quarrels with Elisha Bliss." *AL*, 33(1962): 442–56.

10   HOBEN, J. B. "Mark Twain: On the Writer's Use of Language." *AS*, 32(1956):163–71.

11   HOWELLS, W. D. *My Mark Twain.* New York, 1910.†

12   JONES, A. E. "Mark Twain and Sexuality." *PMLA*, 71(1956):595–616.

13   JONES, A. E. "Mark Twain and the Determinism of *What Is Man?*" *AL* 29(1957):1–17.

14   KAPLAN, Justin, ed. *Mark Twain: A Profile.* New York, 1967.

15   KRAUSE, Sydney J. *Mark Twain as Critic.* Baltimore, 1967.

16   LEARY, Lewis. *Mark Twain.* Minneapolis, 1960.†

17   LEARY, Lewis. "On Writing About Writers: Mark Twain and Howells." *SoR* 4(1968):551–557.

18   LEARY, Lewis. "Standing with Reluctant Feet." In *A Casebook on Mark Twain's Wound.* Ed. by L. Leary. New York, 1962.

19   LETTIS, Richard, William E. MORRIS, and Robert F. McDONNELL, eds. *Huck Finn and His Critics.* New York, 1962. (Text and critical essays by various hands.)†

20   LONG, E. Hudson. *Mark Twain Handbook.* New York, 1957.

21   LORCH, F. W. "Hawaiian Feudalism and Mark Twain's *A Connecticut Yankee in King Arthur's Court*." *AL*, 30(1958):50–66.

22   LORCH, F. W. "Mark Twain's Lecture Tour of 1868–1869: 'The American Vandal Abroad.'" *AL*, 26(1955):515–527.

23   LORCH, F. W. *The Trouble Begins at Eight: Mark Twain's Lecture Tours.* Ames, Iowa, 1968.

24   LUNDY, R. D. "Mark Twain and Italy." *SA*, 4(1958):135–150.

1 LYNN, Kenneth S. *Mark Twain and Southwestern Humor.* Boston, 1960.

2 LYNN, Kenneth S., ed. *Huckleberry Finn: Text, Sources, and Criticism.* New York, 1961. (Essays by various hands.)†

3 McKEITHAN, D. M. *Court Trials in Mark Twain and Other Essays.* The Hague, 1958.

4 MATTSON, J. Stanley. "Mark Twain on War and Peace: the Missouri Rebel and 'The Campaign that Failed.' " *AQ* 20(1968):783–794.

5 PARSONS, C. O. "The Background of *The Mysterious Stranger.*" *AL,* 32(1969):55–74.

6 REED, J. Q. "Mark Twain: West Coast Journalist." *MWQ,* 1(1960):141–161.

7 REES, Robert A., and Richard D. RUST. "Mark Twain's 'The Turning Point of my Life.' " *AL* 40(1969):524–535.

8 RICKELS, Milton. "Samuel Clemens and the Conscience of Comedy." *SoR* 4(1968):558–568.

9 ROGERS, Franklin R. *Mark Twain's Burlesque Patterns as Seen in the Novels and Narratives, 1855–1885.* Dallas, Tex., 1960.

10 ROGERS, Franklin R. "The Road to Reality: Burlesque Travel Literature and Mark Twain's *Roughing It.*" *BNYPL* 67(March, 1963):155–168.

11 SOLOMON, Jack. "*Huckleberry Finn* and the Tradition of *The Odyssey.*" *SAB* 33(1968):11–13.

12 SOLOMON, Roger B. "Mark Twain and Victorian Nostalgia." *Patterns of Commitment in American Literature.* Ed. by M. LaFrance. Toronto, 1967.

13 SOLOMON, Roger B. *Twain and the Image of History.* New Haven, 1961.

14 SCHMIDT, P. "River vs. Town: Mark Twain's *Old Times on the Mississippi.*" *NCF,* 15(1960):95–111.

15 SIMPSON, Claude M., ed. *Twentieth Century Interpretations of The Adventures of Huckleberry Finn.* Englewood Cliffs, N.J., 1968.

16 SMITH, Henry N. "Introduction" to *Adventures of Huckleberry Finn.* Boston, 1958.

17 SMITH, Henry N. "Mark Twain as an Interpreter of the Far West: The Structure of *Roughing It.*" In *The Frontier in Perspective.* Ed. by W. D. Wyman and C. B. Kroeber. Madison, 1957.

18 SMITH, Henry N. *Mark Twain's Fable of Progress: Political and Economic Ideas in "A Connecticut Yankee."* New Brunswick, N.J., 1964.

19 SMITH, Henry N. "Mark Twain's Images of Hannibal: From St. Petersburg to Eseldorf." *TexSE,* 37(1958):3–23.

20 SMITH, Henry N. "*Pudd'nhead Wilson* and After." *MR,* 3(1962):233–253.

1   SPANGLER, George M. *"Pudd'nhead Wilson:* A Parable of Property." *AL* 42(1970):28–37.

2   SPENGERMANN, William C. *Mark Twain and the Backwoods Angel: The Matter of Innocence in the Works of Samuel L. Clemens.* Kent, Ohio, 1967.

3   STONE, Albert E., Jr. *The Innocent Eye: Childhood in Mark Twain's Imagination.* New Haven, 1961.

4   TANNER, T. "The Literary Children of James and Clemens." *NCF*, 16(1961):205–218.

5   TANNER, T. "The Lost America—The Despair of Henry Adams and Mark Twain." *ModA*, 5(1961):299–310.

6   TANNER, T. "Samuel Clemens and the Progress of a Stylistic Rebel." *BAASB*, n.s. 3(1961):31–42.

7   TUCKEY, John S. "Mark Twain's Later Dialogue: The 'Me' and the Machine." *AL* 41(1970):532–542.

8   TUCKEY, John S., ed. *Mark Twain's "The Mysterious Stranger" and the Critics.* Belmont, Calif., 1968.

9   TURNER, Arlin. "Mark Twain and the South: An Affair of Love and Anger." *SoR* 4(1968):493–519.

10 WAGENKNECHT, Edward. *Mark Twain: The Man and His Work.* Rev. ed.   Norman, Okla., 1961.   (Includes section on scholarship.)

11 WIGGER, Anne P. "The Composition of Mark Twain's *Pudd'nhead Wilson and Those Extraordinary Twins:* Chronology and Development." *MP*, 55(1957):93–102.

12 WIGGINS, Robert A. *Mark Twain: Jackleg Novelist.* Seattle, Wash., 1964.

13 WYSONG, Jack P. "Samuel Clemens' Attitude toward the Negro as Demonstrated in *Puddn'head Wilson* and *A Connecticut Yankee*." *XUS* 7(1968):41–57.

14 YATES, N. W. "The 'Counter-Conversion' of Huckleberry Finn." *AL*, 32(1960):1–10.

James Fenimore Cooper (*1789–1851*)

Bibliography

15 SPILLER, R. E., and P. C. BLACKBURN. *A Descriptive Bibliography of the Writings of James Fenimore Cooper.* New York, 1934.

Texts (Cooper's Chief Non-fictional Writings)

16 *Notions of the Americans Picked up by a Travelling Bachelor.* 2 vols. Philadelphia, 1828.

17 *Letter of J. Fenimore Cooper to Gen. Lafayette on the Expenditure of the United States of America.* Paris, 1831.

18 *A Letter to His Countrymen.* New York, 1834.

19 *Sketches of Switzerland. By an American.* 2 vols. Philadelphia, 1836.

1   *Sketches of Switzerland. By an American. Part Second.* 2 vols. Philadelphia, 1836.

2   *Gleanings in Europe.* [France] *By an American.* 2 vols. Philadelphia, 1837.

3   *Gleanings in Europe: England. By an American.* 2 vols. Philadelphia, 1837. (R. E. Spiller has edited the first 4 volumes of *Gleanings* with Introductions for the Oxford UP.)

4   *Gleanings in Europe: Italy. By an American.* 2 vols. Philadelphia, 1838.

5   *The American Democrat; or Hints on the Social and Civic Relations of the United States of America.* Cooperstown, 1838.

6   *The History of the Navy of the United States of America.* 2 vols. Philadelphia, 1839.

7   *The Correspondence of James Fenimore Cooper.* Ed. by James Fenimore Cooper [the grandson]. 2 vols. New Haven, 1929.

8   *The Letters and Journals of James Fenimore Cooper.* 6 vols. Ed. by James F. Beard. Cambridge, Mass., 1967–1969.

Bibliographies

9   BOYNTON, Henry W. *James Fenimore Cooper.* New York, 1951.

10   CLAVEL, M. *Fenimore Cooper, Sa Vie et Son Oeuvre: La Jeunesse (1789–1826).* Aix-en-Provence, 1938.

11   GROSSMAN, James. *James Fenimore Cooper.* New York, 1949.†

12   LOUNSBURY, Thomas R. *James Fenimore Cooper.* Boston, 1882.

13   SPILLER, Robert E. *Fenimore Cooper: Critic of His Times.* New York, 1931.

14   SPILLER, Robert E. *James Fenimore Cooper.* Minneapolis, 1965.†

Critical Studies

15   ABCARIAN, R. "Cooper's Critics and the Realistic Novel." *TSLL,* 8(1966): 33–41.

16   BALL, Roland C. "American Reinterpretations of European Romantic Themes: The Rebel-Hero in Cooper and Melville." In *Proceedings of the IVth Congress of the International Comparative Literature Association.* Ed. by F. Jost. 2 vols. The Hague, 1966.

17   BARBA, P. A. *Cooper in Germany.* Bloomington, Ind., 1914.

18   BOEWE, C. "Cooper's Doctrine of Gifts." *TSL,* 7(1962):27–35.

19   BONNER, E. H. "Cooper and Captain Kidd." *MLN,* 61(1946):21–27.

20   BROWNELL, W. C. *American Prose Masters.* New York, 1909.†

21   CADY, E. H. "The Death of the Agrarian Dream: Fenimore Cooper." In *The Gentleman in America.* Syracuse, N.Y., 1949.

22   CLARK, Harry H. "Fenimore Cooper and Science." *TWA,* 48(1959): 179–204; 49(1960):249–282.

1 CLAVEL, M. *Fenimore Cooper and His Critics.* Aix-en-Provence, 1938.

2 COLLINS, Frank M. "Cooper and the American Dream." *PMLA*, 81(1966): 79–94.

3 CONRAD, Joseph. "Tales of the Sea." In *Notes on Life and Letters.* London, 1921.

4 COWIE, Alexander. "James Fenimore Cooper and the Historical Romance." In *The Rise of the American Novel.* New York, 1951.

5 CUNNINGHAM, M., ed. *James Fenimore Cooper: A Reappraisal.* Cooperstown, N.Y., 1954 (Essays by diverse critics.)

6 DEKKER, George. *James Fenimore Cooper, the American Scott.* New York, 1967.

7 GATES, W. B. "Cooper's Indebtedness to Shakespeare." *PMLA*, 67(1952): 716–731.

8 HASTINGS, G. E. "How Cooper Became a Novelist." *AL*, 12(1940):20–51.

9 HOUSE, K. S. *Cooper's Americans.* Columbus, Ohio, 1965.

10 JONES, H. M. "Prose and Pictures: James Fenimore Cooper." *TSE*, 3(1952):133–154.

11 KIRK, R. "Cooper and the European Puzzle." *CE*, 7(1946):198–207.

12 O'DONNELL, C. "The Moral Basis of Civilization: Cooper's Home Novels." *NCF*, 17(1962):265–273.

13 PARRINGTON, V. L. "James Fenimore Cooper: Critic." In *Main Currents in American Thought.* 3 vols. New York, 1930.

14 PHILBRICK, T. *James Fenimore Cooper and the Development of American Sea Fiction.* Cambridge, Mass., 1961.

15 RINGE, D. *Cooper.* New York, 1964.†

16 ROSS, J. F. *The Social Criticism of Fenimore Cooper.* Berkeley, Calif., 1933.

17 SCUDDER, H. H. "Cooper and the Barbary Coast." *PMLA*, 62(1947): 184–192.

18 SCUDDER, H. H. "What Mr. Cooper Read to His Wife." *SR*, 36(1945): 177–194.

19 SHULENBERGER, A. *Cooper's Theory of Fiction: His Prefaces and Their Relation to His Novels.* Lawrence, Kansas, 1955.

20 SNELL, G. "The Shaper of American Romance." *YR*, 34(1945):482–494.

21 SPILLER, R. E. "Cooper's Notes on Language." *AS*, 4(1929):294–300.

22 VAN DOREN, Carl. *The American Novel: 1780–1939.* Rev. ed. New York, 1940.

23 WALKER, W. S. *James Fenimore Cooper: An Introduction and Interpretation.* New York, 1962.†

24 WALKER, W. S. "Proverbs in the Novels of James Fenimore Cooper." *MF*, 3(1953):99–107.

1 WAPLES, D. *The Whig Myth of Fenimore Cooper.* New Haven, 1938.
2 WHITEHILL, W. M. "Cooper as a Naval Historian." *NYH*, 35(1954): 468–479.
3 WINTERS, Yvor. "Fenimore Cooper, or The Ruins of Time." In *Maule's Curse.* Norfolk, Conn., 1938.
4 WOODRESS, James. "The Fortunes of Cooper in Italy." *SA*, 11(1965): 53–76.

Stephen Crane (1871–1900)

Bibliographies

5 BAUM, Joan H. *Stephen Crane (1871–1900): An Exhibition of His Writings Held in the Columbia University Libraries Sept. 17–Nov. 30, 1956.* New York. 1956.
6 BEEBE, Maurice, and T. A. GULLASON. "Criticism of Stephen Crane: A Selected Checklist with an Index to Studies of Separate Works." *MFS*, 5(Autumn 1959):282–291.
7 GULLASON, Thomas A., ed. *The Complete Novels of Stephen Crane.* Garden City, N.Y., 1967. (Selected Bibliography, pp. 810–821.)
8 WILLIAMS, Ames W., and Vincent STARRETT. *Stephen Crane: A Bibliography.* Glendale, Calif., 1948.

Texts

9 *The Work of Stephen Crane.* Ed. by Wilson Follett. 12 vols. New York, 1925–1926. (Considered standard but very incomplete. See following volumes which supplement this edition.)
10 *The Sullivan County Sketches.* Ed. by Melvin Schoberlin. Syracuse, N.Y., 1949.
11 *Stephen Crane: An Omnibus.* Ed. by Robert W. Stallman. New York, 1952.
12 "Stephen Crane: Some New Stories." Ed. by Robert W. Stallman. *BNYPL*, 61(1957):36–46.
13 *Stephen Crane: Letters.* Ed. by Robert W. Stallman and Lillian Gilkes. New York, 1960.
14 *The Complete Short Stories and Sketches of Stephen Crane.* Ed. with an Introduction by Thomas A. Gullason. Garden City, N.Y., 1963.
15 *Stephen Crane: Uncollected Writings.* Ed. by Olov W. Fryckstedt. Uppsala, 1963.
16 *The War Dispatches of Stephen Crane.* Ed. by Robert W. Stallman and E. R. Hagemann. New York, 1964.
17 *The New York City Sketches of Stephen Crane and Related Pieces.* Ed. by Robert W. Stallman and E. R. Hagemann. New York, 1966.
18 *Poems of Stephen Crane.* Ed. by Joseph Katz. New York, 1966.

1 Crane's *Works*, eds. Fredson Bowers, J. B. Colvert, J. C. Levenson, etc. In accord with Center for Editions . . . (Published so far: *Bowery Tales, Tales of Whilomville*, Crane's *Notebooks*.)

Biographies

2 BEER, Thomas. *Stephen Crane: A Study in American Letters.* Garden City, N.Y., 1927.

3 BERRYMAN, John. *Stephen Crane.* New York, 1950.†

4 GILKES, Lillian. *Cora Crane: A Biography of Mrs. Stephen Crane.* Bloomington, Ind., 1960.

5 STALLMAN, Robert. *Stephen Crane. A Biography.* New York, 1968.

Critical Studies

6 AHNEBRINK, Lars. *The Beginnings of Naturalism in American Fiction: A Study of the Works of Hamlin Garland, Stephen Crane, and Frank Norris with Special Reference to Some European Influences, 1891–1903.* Uppsala, Sweden, 1950.

7 ANDERSON, Warren D. "Homer and Stephen Crane." *NCF*, 19(1964): 77–86.

8 AYERS, Robert W. "W. D. Howells and Stephen Crane: Some Unpublished Letters." *AL*, 28(1957):469–477.

9 BASSAN, Maurice, ed. *Maggie: Text and Context.* Belmont, Calif., 1966. (A collection of critical essays by diverse hands.)†

10 BASSAN, Maurice. "Misery and Society: Some New Perspectives on Stephen Crane's Fiction." *SN*, 35(1963):104–120.

11 BASSAN, Maurice, ed. *Stephen Crane: A Collection of Critical Essays.* Englewood Cliffs, N.J., 1967.†

12 BEEBE, Maurice. "Stephen Crane Number." *MFS*, 5(1959):199–291.

13 BERTHOFF, Warner. *The Ferment of Realism: American Literature, 1884–1919.* New York, 1965.

14 CADY, Edwin H. *Stephen Crane.* New York, 1962.†

15 COLVERT, James B. "The Origins of Stephen Crane's Literary Creed." *TexSE*, 34(1955):179–188.

16 COLVERT, James B. "Structure and Theme in Stephen Crane's Fiction." *MFS*, 5(1959):199–208.

17 COX, James. "*The Pilgrim's Progress* as a Source for Stephen Crane's *The Black Riders*." *AL*, 28(1957):478–487.

18 GEISMAR, Maxwell. *Rebels and Ancestors: The American Novel, 1890–1915.* Boston, 1953.†

19 GILLIS, Everett A. "A Glance at Stephen Crane's Poetry." *PrS*, 28(1954): 43–79.

20 GORDON, Caroline. "Stephen Crane." *Accent*, 9(1949):153–157.

21 GREENFIELD, Stanley B. "The Unmistakable Stephen Crane." *PMLA*, 73(1958):562–572.

1 GULLASON, Thomas A. "The Jamesian Motif in Stephen Crane's Last Novels." *Person*, 42(1961):77–84.

2 GULLASON, Thomas A. "New Light on the Crane-Howells Relationship." *NEQ*, 30(1957):389–392.

3 GULLASON, Thomas A. "Stephen Crane, Anti-Imperialist." *AL*, 30(1958): 237–241.

4 GULLASON, Thomas A. "Stephen Crane's Private War on Yellow Journalism." *HLQ*, 22(1959):201–208.

5 GULLASON, Thomas A. "Tennyson's Influence on Stephen Crane." *N&Q*, 203(1958):164–165.

6 GULLASON, Thomas A. "Thematic Patterns in Stephen Crane's Early Novels." *NCF*, 16(1961):59–67.

7 HAGEMANN, E. R. "Crane's 'Real' War in his Short Stories." *AQ*, 8(1956):356–367.

8 HOFFMAN, Daniel G. *The Poetry of Stephen Crane*. New York, 1957.

9 JOHNSON, George W. "Stephen Crane's Metaphor of Decorum." *PMLA*, 78(1963):250–256.

10 KAZIN, Alfred. *On Native Grounds: An Interpretation of Modern American Prose Literature*. New York, 1942.†

11 KINDILIEN, Carlin T. *American Poetry in the Eighteen Nineties*. Providence, R.I., 1956.

12 KINDILIEN, Carlin T. "Stephen Crane and the 'Savage Philosophy' of Olive Schreiner." *BUSE*, 3(1957):97–107.

13 KWIAT, J. J. "The Newspaper Experience: Crane, Norris, and Dreiser." *NCF*, 8(1953):99–117.

14 KWIAT, J. J. "Stephen Crane and Painting." *AQ*, 4(1952):331–338.

15 LaFRANCE, Marston. "Stephen Crane's *Private Fleming: His Various Battles*." In *Patterns of Commitment in American Literature*. Ed. by Marston LaFrance. Toronto, 1967.

16 LEAVER, Florence. "Isolation in the Work of Stephen Crane." *SAQ*, 61(1962):521–532.

17 LEVENSON, J. C. "Stephen Crane." In *Major Writers of America*. Ed. by Perry Miller. New York, 1962.

18 LIEBLING, A. J. "The Dollars Damned Him." *NY*, 37(Aug. 5, 1961): 48–60, 63–66, 69–72.

19 LINSON, Corwin K. *My Stephen Crane*. Ed. by Edwin H. Cady. Syracuse, N.Y., 1958.

20 LOWELL, Amy. "Introduction." In *The Work of Stephen Crane*, Vol. 6. New York, 1926.

21 MENCKEN, H. L. "Introduction." In *The Work of Stephen Crane*, Vol. 10. New York, 1962.

22 MORGAN, H. Wayne. "Stephen Crane: The Ironic Hero." In *Writers in Transition: Seven Americans*. New York, 1963.

23 NELSON, Harland S. "Crane's Achievement as Poet." *TSLL*, 4(1963): 564–582.

1 NYE, Russel B. "Stephen Crane as a Social Critic." *ModQ*, 11(Summer, 1940):48–54.

2 O'DONNELL, Thomas F. "A Note on the Reception of Crane's The Black Riders." *AL*, 24(1952):233–235.

3 OSBORN, Scott C. "The 'Rivalry-Chivalry' of Richard Harding Davis and Stephen Crane." *AL*, 28(1956):50–61.

4 ØVERLAND, Orm. "The Impressionism of Stephen Crane: A Study in Style and Technique." In *Americana Norwegica*. Ed. by Sigmund Skard and H. H. Wasser. Philadelphia, 1966.

5 PIZER, Donald. "Crane Reports Garland on Howells." *MLN*, 70(1955):37–38.

6 PIZER, Donald. "Romantic Individualism in Garland, Norris, and Crane." *AQ*, 10(1958):463–475.

7 QUINN, A. H., ed. *The Literature of the American People.* New York, 1951.

8 RAYMOND, Thomas L. *Stephen Crane.* Newark, N.J., 1923.

9 SOLOMON, Eric. *Stephen Crane, From Parody to Realism.* Cambridge, Mass., 1966.

10 STARRETT, Vincent. "An Estimate of Stephen Crane." *SR*, 28(1920):405–413.

11 STEVENSON, John W. "The Literary Reputation of Stephen Crane." *SAQ*, 51(1951):287–300.

12 VAN DOREN, Carl. "Stephen Crane." *AmMerc*, 1(1924):11–14.

13 WALCUTT, Charles C. *American Literary Naturalism, A Divided Stream.* Minneapolis, 1956.

14 WEGELIN, Christof. "Crane's 'A Man Said to the Universe'." *Expl*, 20(1961):item 9.

15 WELLS, H. G. "Stephen Crane: From an English Standpoint." *NAR*, 171(1900):233–242.

16 WEST, Ray B., Jr. "Stephen Crane: Author in Transition." *AL*, 34(1962):215–228.

17 WESTBROOK, Max. "Stephen Crane: The Pattern of Affirmation." *NCF*, 14(1959):219–229.

18 WESTBROOK, Max. "Stephen Crane's Poetry: Perspective and Arrogance." *BuR*, 11, iv(Dec. 1963):24–34.

19 WESTBROOK, Max. "Stephen Crane's Social Ethic." *AQ*, 14(1962):587–596.

20 ZIFF, Larzer. *The American 1890's: Life and Times of a Lost Generation.* New York, 1966.†

Emily Dickinson (1830–1886)

Bibliographies

21 BUCKINGHAM, Willis, compiler. *Emily Dickinson, An Annotated Bibliography.* (Includes scholarship through 1968.) Ind., 1970.

MAJOR AMERICAN WRITERS **25**

1 SPILLER, R. E. et al. *Literary History of the United States*, Vol. 3: *Bibliography*. New York, 1948. *Supplement.* Ed. by Richard Ludwig. New York, 1959.
2 CLENDENNING, Sheila T. *Emily Dickinson: A Bibliography: 1850–1966.* Kent, Ohio, 1968.

Concordance

3 ROSENBAUM, S. P., ed. *A Concordance to the Poems of Emily Dickinson.* Ithaca, N.Y., 1964.

Texts

4 *The Poems of Emily Dickinson, Including Variant Readings Critically Compared with All Known Manuscripts.* Ed. by Thomas H. Johnson. 3 vols. Cambridge, Mass., 1955.
5 *The Letters of Emily Dickinson.* Ed. by Thomas H. Johnson. 3 vols. Cambridge, Mass., 1958.

Biographies

6 BIANCHI, M. Dickinson. *Emily Dickinson Face to Face.* Boston, 1932.
7 BIANCHI, M. Dickinson. *The Life and Letters of Emily Dickinson.* Boston, 1924.
8 BINGHAM, M. T. *Ancestor's Brocades: The Literary Debut of Emily Dickinson.* New York, 1945.
9 BINGHAM, M. T. *Emily Dickinsons's Home.* New York, 1955. (Letters of Edward Dickinson and his family.)†
10 JOHNSON, T. H. *Emily Dickinson: An Interpretative Biography.* Cambridge, Mass., 1955.†
11 LEYDA, Jay. *The Years and Hours of Emily Dickinson.* 2 vols. New Haven, 1960.
12 PATTERSON, R. *The Riddle of Emily Dickinson.* Boston, 1951.
13 POLLITT, J. *Emily Dickinson: The Human Background of Her Poetry.* New York, 1930.
14 TAGGARD, G. *The Life and Mind of Emily Dickinson.* New York, 1930.
15 WARD, T. *The Capsule of the Mind: Chapters in the Life of Emily Dickinson.* Cambridge, Mass., 1961.

Critical Studies

16 ADAMS, R. P. "Dickinson Concrete." *ESQ*, 44(1966):31–35.
17 ADAMS, R. P. "Pure Poetry: Emily Dickinson." *TSE*, 7(1957):133–152.

1 AIKEN, C. "Emily Dickinson." *Dial*, 76(1924):301–308.

2 ALLEN, G. W. "Emily Dickinson." In *American Prosody*. New York, 1935.

3 ANDERSON, C. R. *Emily Dickinson's Poetry: The Stairway of Surprise.* New York, 1960.†

4 ANDERSON, P. W. "The Metaphysical Mirth of Emily Dickinson." *GaR*, 20(1966):72–83.

5 BIRDSALL, V. O. "Emily Dickinson's Intruder in the Soul." *AL*, 37(1965): 54–64.

6 BLACKMUR, R. P. "Emily Dickinson." In *Major Writers of America*, Vol. 2. Ed. by Perry Miller. New York, 1956. (See also *KR*, 18[1956]: 224–237.)

7 BLACKMUR, R. P. "Emily Dickinson: Notes on Prejudice and Fact." *SoR*, 3(1937):325–347.

8 BLAKE, C. R., and Carlton F. WELLS, eds. *The Recognition of Emily Dickinson: Selected Criticism since 1890.* Ann Arbor, 1964.

9 BOGAN, Louise, Archibald MACLEISH, and Richard WILBUR. *Emily Dickinson: Three Views.* Amherst, Mass., 1960.

10 CAMBON, G. "Emily Dickinson and the Crisis of Self-Reliance," in *Transcendentalism and its Legacy*. Ed. by M. Simon and T. Thornton. Ann Arbor, 1966.

11 CAPPS, J. L. *Emily Dickinson's Reading, 1836–1886.* Cambridge, Mass., 1966.

12 CHASE, Richard. *Emily Dickinson.* New York, 1951.†

13 CURTIS, J. R. "Edward Taylor and Emily Dickinson: Voices and Visions." *SUS*, 7(1964):159–167.

14 DAVIDSON, F. "'This Consciousness': Emerson and Dickinson." *ESQ*, 44(1966):2–7.

15 DUNCAN, D. *Emily Dickinson.* Edinburgh, 1965.

16 EMBLEN, D. L. "A Comment on 'Structural Patterns in the Poetry of Emily Dickinson'." *AL*, 37(1965):64–65.

17 ENGLAND, M. W. "Emily Dickinson and Isaac Watts: Puritan Hymnodists." *BNYPL*, 69(1965):83–116.

18 FORD, Thomas W. "Emily Dickinson and the Civil War." *UR*, 31(1965): 199–203.

19 FORD, Thomas W. *Heaven Beguiles the Tired: Death in the Poetry of Emily Dickinson.* University, Ala., 1966.

20 FRANKLIN, Ralph. *The Editing of Emily Dickinson: A Reconsideration.* Madison, Wis., 1967.

21 FRYE, N. "Emily Dickinson." In *Major Writers of America*, vol. 2. Ed. by Perry Miller. New York, 1962.

22 GELPI, A. J. *Emily Dickinson, The Mind of the Poet.* Cambridge, Mass., 1965.

23 GRIFFITH, C. *The Long Shadow: Emily Dickinson's Tragic Poetry.* Princeton, 1964.†

1 HIGGINS, D. J. M. "Twenty-five Poems by Emily Dickinson: Unpublished Variant Versions." *AL*, 38(1966):1–21.

2 HIGGINS, David J. *Portrait of Emily Dickinson: The Poet and Her Prose.* New Brunswick, New Jersey, 1967.

3 HIGGINSON, T. W. "Emily Dickinson's Letters." *AtlM*, 68(1891):444–456. (An important early essay.)

4 HOWARD, William. "Emily Dickinson's Poetic Vocabulary." *PMLA*, 72(1957):225–248.

5 LAVERTY, C. D. "Structural Patterns in Emily Dickinson's Poetry." *ESQ*, 44(1966):12–17.

6 LINDBERG-SEIJERSTED, Brita. *The Voice of the Poet: Aspects of Style in the Poetry of Emily Dickinson.* Cambridge, Mass., 1968.†

7 LUBBERS, Klaus. *Emily Dickinson: The Critical Revolution.* Ann Arbor, Mich., 1968.

8 MATTHIESSEN, F. O. "The Problem of the Private Poet." *KR*, 7(1945): 584–597.

9 MERIDETH, Robert. "Emily Dickinson and the Acquisitive Society." *NEQ*, 37(1964):435–452.

10 MILLER, Ruth. *The Poetry of Emily Dickinson.* Middletown, Conn., 1968.

11 MOLDENHAUER, J. J. "Emily Dickinson's Ambiguity: Notes on Technique." *ESQ*, 44(1966):35–44.

12 MONTEIRO, G. "Traditional Ideas in Dickinson's 'I Felt a Funeral in My Brain'." *MLN*, 75(1960):656–663.

13 NODA, Hisashi. "Emily Dickinson's Poetry: An Essay on the Symbols of 'Death'." *KAL*, 6(1963):23–29.

14 PICKARD, J. B. *Emily Dickinson: An Introduction and Interpretation.* New York, 1967.†

15 PORTER, D. T. "Emily Dickinson: The Formative Years." *MR*, 6(1965): 559–569. (Followed, pp. 570–580, by a reprint of T. W. Higginson's 1862 "Letter to a Young Contributor" in the *Atlantic*.)

16 PORTER, David T. *The Art of Emily Dickinson's Early Poetry.* Cambridge Mass., 1966.

17 RABE, O. H. "Emily Dickinson as Mystic." *ColQ*, 14(1966):280–288.

18 RANSOM, J. G. "Emily Dickinson." *PUSA*, 15(1956):5–20.

19 ROSENBAUM, S. P. "Emily Dickinson and the Machine." *SB*, 18(1965): 207–227.

20 SCOTT, W. T. "Emily Dickinson and Samuel Bowles." In *Exiles and Fabrications.* New York, 1961.

21 SEWALL, R. B. *The Lyman Letters: New Light on Emily Dickinson and Her Family.* Amherst, Mass., 1965.

22 SEWALL, R. B., ed. *Emily Dickinson: A Collection of Critical Essays.* With Introduction. Englewood Cliffs, N.J., 1963.†

23 SHERWOOD, W. R. *Circumference and Circumstance: Stages in the Mind and Art of Emily Dickinson.* New York, 1968.

1 SANDEEN, Ernest. "Delight Deterred by Retrospect: Emily Dickinson's Late-Summer Poems." *NEQ*, 40(1967):483–500.

2 STAMM, E. P. "Emily Dickinson: Poetry and Punctuation." *SatR*, 46(March 30, 1963):26–27, 74.

3 TATE, Allen. "New England Culture and Emily Dickinson." *Symposium*, 3(1932):206–226. (Also in Tate's *The Man of Letters in the Modern World*. New York, 1955.)

4 WAGGONER, H. H. "Emily Dickinson: The Transcendent Self." *Criticism*, 7(1965):297–334.

5 WARREN, A. "Emily Dickinson." *SR*, 65(1957):565–586.

6 WELLS, Anna Mary. "Was Emily Dickinson Psychotic?" *AI*, 19(1962): 309–321.

7 WELLS, H. W. *Introduction to Emily Dickinson*. New York, 1947.

8 WHEATCROFT, J. "Emily Dickinson's Poetry and Jonathan Edwards on the Will." *BuR*, 10(1961):102–127.

9 WHICHER, G. F. *This Was a Poet: A Critical Biography of Emily Dickinson*. New York, 1938.†

10 WILSON, S. M. "Emily Dickinson and Twentieth-Century Poetry of Sensibility." *AL*, 36(1964):349–358.

11 WILSON, S. M. "Structural Patterns in the Poetry of Emily Dickinson." *AL*, 35(1963):53–59.

12 WINTERS, Yvor. "Emily Dickinson and the Limits of Judgment." In *Maule's Curse*. Norfolk, Conn., 1938.

Ralph Waldo Emerson (1803–1882)

Bibliographies

13 BOOTH, R. A., and Roland STROMBERG. "A Bibliography of Ralph Waldo Emerson, 1908–1920." *BB*, 19(1948):180–183.

14 BRYER, J. R., and R. A. REES. *A Checklist of Emerson Criticism, 1951–1961, with a Detailed Index*. Hartford, 1964.

15 COOKE, G. W. *A Bibliography of Ralph Waldo Emerson*. Boston, 1908.

16 STOVALL, Floyd. "Emerson." In *Eight American Authors: A Review of Research and Criticism*. New York, 1956. Supplemented by J. C. Mathews in 1963 printing.†

Concordance

17 HUBBELL, G. S. *A Concordance of the Poems of Ralph Waldo Emerson*. New York, 1932.

Texts

1 *The Complete Works of Ralph Waldo Emerson.* Ed. by E. W. Emerson. Centenary Edition, 12 vols. Boston, 1903–1904.
2 *Journals of Ralph Waldo Emerson.* Ed. by E. W. Emerson and W. E. Forbes. 10 vols. Boston, 1909–1914.
3 *The Letters of Ralph Waldo Emerson.* Ed. by R. L. Rusk. 6 vols. New York, 1939.
4 *Selections from Emerson's Prose and Poetry.* Ed. by S. E. Whicher. Boston, 1957.
5 *The Early Lectures of Ralph Waldo Emerson.* Ed. by S. E. Whicher and R. E. Spiller. 2 vols. Cambridge, Mass., 1959–1964.
6 *Dante's Vita Nuova*, trans. by Ralph Waldo Emerson. Ed. by J. C. Mathews. Chapel Hill, N.C., 1960.
7 *The Journals and Miscellaneous Notebooks of Ralph Waldo Emerson.* Ed. by W. H. Gilman, A. R. Ferguson, G. P. Clark, M. R. Davis, M. M. Sealts, Jr., Harrison Hayford, and Ralph H. Orth. Cambridge, Mass., 1960– . Vol. VII, 1838–1842, ed. by A. W. Plumstead and others, 1970.
8 "Thirty-Three Unpublished Letters of Ralph Waldo Emerson." Ed. by William White. *AL*, 33(1961):159–178.
9 *English Traits.* Ed. with Introduction by Howard M. Jones. Cambridge, Mass., 1966.

Biography

10 CABOT, J. E. *A Memoir of Ralph Waldo Emerson.* 2 vols. Boston, 1887. (The "official" life, now superseded by that of Rusk.)
11 FIRKINS, Oscar. *Ralph Waldo Emerson.* Boston, 1915.
12 RUSK, R. L. *The Life of Ralph Waldo Emerson.* New York, 1949.
13 WOODBERRY, George E. *Life of Emerson.* New York, 1907.

Critical Studies

14 ADAMS, R. P. "Emerson and the Organic Metaphor." *PMLA*, 69(1954): 117–130.
15 ADKINS, Nelson F. "Emerson and the Bardic Tradition." *PMLA*, 63(1948):662–677.
16 ALLEN, G. W. *American Prosody.* New York, 1935.
17 ANDERSON, J. Q. "Emerson and 'Manifest Destiny'." *BPLQ*, 7(1955): 23–33.
18 ANZILOTTI, Rolando. "Emerson in Italia." *RLMC*, 11(1958):70–80.
19 ARNOLD, Matthew. "Emerson." In *Discourses in America.* London, 1885.
20 ARVIN, Newton. "The House of Pain: Emerson and the Tragic Sense." *HudR*, 12(1959):37–53.
21 BEACH, J. W. 'Emerson and Evolution." *UTQ*, 3(1934):474–497.

1 BERRY, E. G. *Emerson's Plutarch*. Cambridge, Mass., 1961.

2 BIRDSALL, R. D. "Emerson and the Church of Rome." *AL*, 31(1959): 273–281.

3 BISHOP, Jonathan. *Emerson on the Soul*. Cambridge, Mass., 1964.

4 BLAIR, Walter, and Clarence FAUST. "Emerson's Literary Method." *MP*, 42(1944):79–95.

5 BLOOM, Robert. "Irving Babbitt's Emerson," *NEQ*, 30(1957):448–473.

6 BODE, Carl, ed. *Selections* [from diverse critics on Emerson]. New York, 1968.

7 BRASWELL, William. "Melville as a Critic of Emerson." *AL*, 9(1937): 317–334.

8 BRAWNER, J. P. "Emerson's Debt to Italian Art." *WVUPP*, 8(1951):49–58.

9 BRITTIN, N. A. "Emerson and the Metaphysical Poets." *AL*, 8(1936):1–21.

10 BRODERICK, John C. "Emerson and Moorfield Storey: A Lost Journal Found." *AL*, 38(1966):177–186.

11 BROWN, Stuart Gerry. "Emerson." *UKCR*, 15(1948):27–37.

12 BROWN, Stuart Gerry. "Emerson's Platonism." *NEQ*, 18(1945):325–345.

13 BROWNELL, W. C. "Emerson." In *American Prose Masters*. New York, 1909.

14 BRUEL, Andrée. *Emerson et Thoreau*. Paris, 1929.

15 CAMERON, K. W. *A Commentary on Emerson's Early Lectures (1833–1836)*, with an Index-Concordance. Hartford, 1962.

16 CAMERON, K. W. *An Emerson Index: Names, Exempla, Sententiae, Symbols, Words and Motifs in Selected Notebooks of Ralph Waldo Emerson*. Hartford, 1958.

17 CAMERON, K. W. *Emerson the Essayist*. 2 vols. Raleigh, N.C., 1945.

18 CAMERON, K. W. *Ralph Waldo Emerson's Reading: A Corrected Edition, with Photographs of Literary Concord, Emerson, and His Family*. Hartford, 1962.

19 CAMERON, K. W. *The Transcendentalists and Minerva*. 3 vols. Hartford, 1958.

20 CANBY, H. S. "Emerson." In *Classic Americans*. New York, 1931.

21 CARPENTER, F. I. *Emerson and Asia*. Cambridge, Mass., 1930.

22 CARPENTER, F. I. *Emerson Handbook*. New York, 1953.

23 CARPENTER, H. C. "Emerson, Eliot, and the Elective System." *NEQ*, 24(1951):13–34.

24 CESTRE, Charles. "Le Romantisme d'Emerson." *RAA* 7(1929):1–18, 113–131.

25 CHAPMAN, J. J. "Emerson." In *Emerson and Other Essays*. New York, 1898.

1 CHARVAT, William. *Emerson's American Lecture Engagements: A Chronological List.* New York, 1961.
2 CHRISTY, Arthur. *The Orient in American Transcendentalism: A Study of Emerson, Thoreau, and Alcott.* New York, 1932.
3 CLARK, Harry H. "Conservative and Mediatory Emphases in Emerson's Thought." In *Transcendentalism and Its Legacy.* Ed. by Myron Simons, and T. H. Parsons. Ann Arbor, Mich., 1966.
4 CLARK, Harry H. "Emerson and Science." *PQ*, 10(1931):225–260.
5 CONNOR, F. W. *Cosmic Optimism.* Gainesville, Fla., 1949. (On science.)
6 COOK, R. L. "Emerson and Frost: A Parallel of Seers." *NEQ*, 31(1958): 200–217.
7 CORY, Arthur M. "Humor in Emerson's Journals." *TexSE*, 34(1955): 114–124.
8 COWAN, Michael H. *City of the West: Emerson, America, and Urban Metaphor.* New Haven, 1967.
9 DAVIDSON, Frank. "Emerson and the Double Consciousness." *ER*, 3(1960):1–15.
10 DODERER, Hans. "Der Junge Emerson und Deutschland." *GRM*, 36(1955):147–161.
11 EMERSON, E. W. *Emerson in Concord: A Memoir.* Boston, 1890.
12 *The Emerson Society Quarterly.* Ed. by K. W. Cameron. Hartford, 1955– .
13 FALK, R. P. "Emerson and Shakespeare." *PMLA*, 56(1941):532–543.
14 FEIDELSON, Charles. "Toward Melville: Some Versions of Emerson." In *Symbolism and American Literature.* Chicago, 1953.
15 FERGUSON, J. De L. *American Literature in Spain.* New York, 1916.
16 FLANAGAN, J. T. "Emerson as a Critic of Fiction." *PQ*, 15(1936):30–45.
17 FOERSTER, Norman. "Emerson." In *American Criticism: A Study in Literary Theory from Poe to the Present.* Boston, 1928.
18 FOERSTER, Norman. "Emerson." In *Nature in American Literature: Studies in the Modern View of Nature.* New York, 1923.
19 FRANCIS, Richard L. "Archangel in the Pleached Garden: Emerson's Poetry." *ELH*, 33(1966):461–472.
20 FRANCIS, Richard L. "The Architectonics of Emerson's *Nature*." *AQ*, 19(1967):39–52.
21 FROST, Robert. "On Emerson." *Daedalus*, 88(1959):712–718.
22 GERBER, J. C. "Emerson and the Political Economists." *NEQ*, 22(1949): 336–357.
23 GODDARD, H. C. *Studies in New England Transcendentalism.* New York, 1908.
24 GOHDES, C. L. F. *The Periodicals of American Transcendentalism.* Durham, N.C., 1931.

1 GONNAUD, Maurice. *Individu et Société dans L'Oeuvre de Ralph Waldo Emerson: Essai de Biographie Spirituelle.* Paris, 1964.

2 GORELY, Jean. "Emerson's Theory of Poetry." *Poetry R*, 22(1931):263–273.

3 GRAY, H. D. *Emerson: A Statement of New England Transcendentalism as Expressed in the Philosophy of Its Chief Exponent.* Stanford, Calif., 1917.

4 GREENLEAF, Richard. "Emerson and Wordsworth." *S&S*, 22(1958): 218–230.

5 GROSS, S. L. "Emerson and Poetry." *SAQ*, 54(1955):82–94.

6 HARRISON, J. S. *The Teachers of Emerson.* New York, 1910.

7 HENDRICK, George. "Influence of Thoreau and Emerson on Gandhi's Satyagraha." *GM*, 3(1959):165–178.

8 HOLMES, O. W. *Ralph Waldo Emerson.* Boston, 1885.

9 HOPKINS, Vivian C. "Emerson and Bacon." *AL*, 29(1958):408–430.

10 HOPKINS, Vivian C. "Emerson and Cudworth: Plastic Nature and Transcendental Art." *AL*, 23(1951):80–98.

11 HOPKINS, Vivian C. "The Influence of Goethe on Emerson's Aesthetic Theory." *PQ*, 27(1948):325–344.

12 HOPKINS, Vivian C. *Spires of Form: A Study of Emerson's Aesthetic Theory.* Cambridge, Mass., 1951.

13 HOTSON, Clarence. "Emerson and Swedenborg." *NCM*, 140(1930): 274–277.

14 HUTCHISON, W. R. *The Transcendental Ministers: Church Reform in the New England Renaissance.* New Haven, 1959.†

15 JAMES, Henry. "Emerson." In *Partial Portraits.* London, 1899.

16 JAMIESON, P. F. "Emerson in the Adirondacks." *NYH*, 39(1958):215–237.

17 JONES, Howard Mumford. *Emerson Once More: The Ware Lecture.* Boston, 1953.

18 JONES, Joseph. "Emerson and Bergson on the Cosmic," *CL*, 1(1949):63–72.

19 JORGENSON, C. E. "Emerson's Paradise under the Shadow of Swords." *PQ*, 11(1932):274–292.

20 KELLER, Hans. *Emerson in Frankreich Wirkungen und Parallelen.* Giessen, 1932.

21 KLEINFIELD, H. L. "The Structure of Emerson's 'Death'," *BNYPL*, 65(1961):47–64.

22 KLOECKNER, A. J. "Intellect and Moral Sentiment in Emerson's Opinions of 'The Meaner Kinds' of Men." *AL*, 30(1958):322–338.

23 KREYMBORG, Alfred. "The Intoxicated Emerson." In *Our Singing Strength.* New York, 1929.

24 KWIAT, J. J. "Robert Henri and the Emerson-Whitman Tradition." *PMLA*, 71(1956):617–636.

25 LAUTER, Paul. "Emerson's Revisions of *Essays* (First Series)." *AL*, 33(1961):143–158.

1 LAUTER, Paul. "Truth and Nature: Emerson's Use of Two Complex Words." *ELH*, 27(1960):66–85.

2 LEE, R. F. "Emerson through Kierkegaard: Toward a Definition of Emerson's Theory of Communication." *ELH*, 24(1957):229–248.

3 LINDEMAN, E. C. "Emerson's Pragmatic Mood." *ASch*, 16(1946–1947): 57–64.

4 LOWELL, J. R. "Emerson, the Lecturer." In *My Study of Windows*. Boston, 1871.

5 MARCHAND, Ernest. "Emerson and the Frontier." *AL*, 3(1931):149–174.

6 MARKS, Emerson R. "Victor Cousin and Emerson." In *Transcendentalism and its Legacy*. Ed. by Myron Simons and T. H. Parsons. Ann Arbor, Mich., 1966.

7 MASONS, G. R. "Ralph Waldo Emerson." In *Great American Liberals*. Boston, 1956.

8 MATTHIESSEN, F. O. "From Emerson to Thoreau." In *American Renaissance: Art and Expression in the Age of Emerson and Whitman*. New York, 1941.

9 McCORMICK, J. O. "Emerson's Theory of Human Greatness." *NEQ*, 26(1953):291–314.

10 McELDERRY, B. R., Jr. "Emerson's Second Address on the American Scholar." *Person*, 39(1958):361–372.

11 McEUEN, K. A. "Emerson's Rhymes." *AL*, 20(1948):31–42.

12 McMULLEN, Haynes. "Ralph Waldo Emerson and the Libraries." *LQ*, 25(1955):152–162.

13 McQUISTON, Raymer. "The Relation of Ralph Waldo Emerson to Public Affairs." *Bulletin of the University of Kansas* 24, viii(1923):1–63.

14 METZGER, Charles R. *Emerson and Greenough: Transcendental Pioneers of an American Aesthetic*. Berkeley, Calif., 1954.

15 MICHAUD, Régis. *Emerson: The Enraptured Yankee*, trans. by George Boas. New York, 1930.

16 MICHAUD, Régis. *L'Esthétique d'Emerson*. Paris, 1927.

17 MILLER, Perry. "Emersonian Genius and the American Democracy." *NEQ*, 36(1953):27–44.

18 MOORE, J. B. "Emerson on Wordsworth." *PMLA*, 41(1926):179–192.

19 MORE, P. E. "Emerson." In *The Cambridge History of American Literature*. New York, 1917. (Repr. in *Shelburne Essays, Eleventh Series*. Boston, 1921.)

20 NICOLOFF, P. L. *Emerson on Race and History: An Examination of "English Traits."* New York, 1961.

21 ODELL, A. T. *La Doctrine Sociale d'Emerson*. Paris, 1931.

22 OSTRANDER, G. G. "Emerson, Thoreau, and John Brown," *MVHR*, 39(1953):713–726.

23 PADOVER, S. K. "Ralph Waldo Emerson: The Moral Voice in Politics." *PSQ*, 74(1959):334–350.

1 PARRINGTON, V. L. "Emerson, Transcendental Critic." In *The Romantic Revolution in America*. New York, 1927.

2 PAUL, Sherman. *Emerson's Angle of Vision: Man and Nature in American Experience*. Cambridge, Mass., 1952.

3 PEARCE, R. H. *The Continuity of American Poetry*. Princeton, 1961.†

4 PERRY, Bliss. *Emerson Today*. Princeton, 1931.

5 PETTIGREW, R. C. "Emerson and Milton." *AL*, 3(1931):45–59.

6 POLLOCK, R. C. "A Re-appraisal of Emerson." *Thought*, 32(1957):86–132.

7 POMMER, H. F. "The Contents and Basis of Emerson's Belief in Compensation." *PMLA*, 77(1962):248–253.

8 PORTE, Joel. *Emerson and Thoreau; Transcendentalists in Conflict*. Middletown, Conn., 1966.

9 REID, Alfred S. "Emerson and Bushnell: Forerunners of Jamesian Pragmatism." *FurmS*, 13, i(1965):18–30.

10 ROBERTS, J. Russell. "Emerson's Debt to the Seventeenth Century." *AL*, 21(1949):298–310.

11 ROOS, Jacques. "Ce que Maeterlinck doit à l'Amérique." *BFLS*, 37(1958): 197–208.

12 RUCHAMES, Louis. "Two Forgotten Addresses by Ralph Waldo Emerson." *AL*, 28(1957):425–433.

13 RUSK, Ralph L. "Emerson and the Stream of Experience." *CE*, 14(1953): 373–379; *EJ*, 42(1953):181–187.

14 SANTAYANA, George. "Emerson." In *Interpretations of Poetry and Religion*. New York, 1957.

15 SCUDDER, Townsend, III. "A Chronological List of Emerson's Lectures on His British Tour of 1847–1848." *PMLA*, 51(1936):243–248.

16 SCUDDER, Townsend, III. "Emerson in London and the London Lectures." *AL*, 8(1936):22–36.

17 SCUDDER, Townsend, III. "Emerson's British Lecture Tour, 1847–1848." *AL*, 7(1935):15–36, 166–180.

18 SEALTS, Merton M., Jr., and Alfred R. FERGUSON, eds. *Emerson's Nature—Origin, Growth, Meaning*. New York, 1969.

19 SHERMAN, S. P. "The Emersonian Liberation." In *The Americans*. New York, 1924.

20 SILVER, R. G. "Emerson as Abolitionist." *NEQ*, 6(1933):154–158.

21 SOWDER, William J. *Emerson's Impact on the British Isles and Canada*. Charlottesville, Va., 1966.

22 SOWDER, William J. "Emerson's Reviewers and Commentators: Nineteenth-Century Periodical Criticism." *ESQ*, 53(1958):1–51.

23 SPILLER, R. E. "Emerson." In *Literary History of the United States*. New York, 1948.

24 STAFFORD, William T. "Emerson and the James Family." *AL*, 24(1953): 433–461.

1 STENERSON, Douglas C. "Emerson and the Agrarian Tradition." *JHI*, 14(1953):95–115.
2 STEPHEN, Leslie. "Emerson." In *Studies of a Biographer*. London, 1902.
3 STRAUCH, Carl F. "Emerson and the Doctrine of Sympathy." *SIR*, 6(1967):152–174. (Mr. Strauch has published in periodicals a large number of valuable studies of individual poems of Emerson, based on his dissertation of 1946 at Yale preparing for "Critical and Variorum Edition of Emerson's Poems.")
4 STRAUCH, Carl F. "Introduction" to Emerson. In *American Literary Masters*. Ed. by Charles Anderson. New York, 1965.
5 STRAUCH, Carl F. "The Year of Emerson's Poetic Maturity: 1834." *PQ*, 34(1955):353–377.
6 SUTCLIFFE, E. G. *Emerson's Theories of Literary Expression*. Urbana, Ill., 1923.
7 THOMPSON, F. T. "Emerson and Carlyle." *SP*, 24(1927):438–453.
8 THOMPSON, F. T. "Emerson's Indebtedness of Coleridge." *SP*, 23(1926):55–76.
9 THOMPSON, F. T. "Emerson's Theory and Practice of Poetry." *PMLA*, 43(1928):1170–1184.
10 TRUEBLOOD, D. Elton. "The Influence of Emerson's 'Divinity School Address'." *HTR*, 32(1939):41–56.
11 USTICK, W. L. "Emerson's Debt to Montaigne." *Washington University Studies, Humanistic Series*, 4th ser., 9, ii(1921):245–262.
12 VAN WESEP, H. B. "Ralph Waldo Emerson: Gentle Iconoclast." In *Seven Sages: The Story of American Philosophy*. New York, 1960.
13 WAHR, F. B. *Emerson and Goethe*. Ann Arbor, Mich., 1915.
14 WELLEK, Rene. "Emerson and German Philosophy." *NEQ*, 16(1943):41–62.
15 WELLEK, Rene. "Emerson's Literary Theory and Criticism." In *Worte und Werte*. Ed. by G. Erdmann and A. Eichstaedt. Berlin, 1961.
16 WHICHER, Stephen E. "Emerson's Tragic Sense." *ASch*, 22(1953):285–292.
17 WHICHER, Stephen E. *Freedom and Fate: An Inner Life of Ralph Waldo Emerson*. Philadelphia, 1953.†
18 WHICHER, Stephen E. "Introduction" to *Selections from Ralph Waldo Emerson*. Boston, 1957.
19 WHITAKER, T. R. "The Riddle of Emerson's 'Sphinx'." *AL*, 27(1955):179–195.
20 WILLIAMS, S. T. "Emerson: An Affirmation." *TSL*, 2(1957):41–50.
21 WRIGHT, Conrad. "Emerson, Barzillai Frost, and the Divinity School Address." *HTR*, 49(1956):19–43.
22 WRIGHT, Nathalia. "Ralph Waldo Emerson and Horatio Greenough." *HLB*, 12(1958):91–116.

1 YAHAGI, Hiromichi. "The Position of Ralph Waldo Emerson in the Formation of Americanism." *TDK*, 45(1960):85–146. [In Japanese.]
2 ZINK, Harriet R. "Emerson's Use of the Bible." *University of Nebraska Studies in Language, Literature, and Criticism*, No. 14. Lincoln, Neb., 1935.

Hamlin Garland (1860–1940)

Texts

3 *The Works of Hamlin Garland.* 12 vols. New York, 1922.
4 *Crumbling Idols.* Ed. with Introduction by Jane Johnson. Cambridge, Mass., 1960.†
5 *Hamlin Garland's Diaries.* Ed. by Donald Pizer. San Marino, Calif., 1965.

Biographies

6 HOLLOWAY, Jean. *Hamlin Garland: A Biography.* Austin, Tex., 1960.
7 MANE, Robert. *Hamlin Garland: L'Homme et L'Oeuvre.* Paris, 1967.
8 PIZER, Donald. "A Bibliography of Hamlin Garland." *American Literary Realism.* I(1967):45–51.
9 PIZER, Donald. *Hamlin Garland's Early Work and Career.* Berkeley, Calif., 1960.
10 PIZER, Donald. "Hamlin Garland's *A Son of the Middle Border:* Autobiography as 'Art'." In *Essays in American Literature Presented to Bruce McElderry, Jr.* Athens, Ohio, 1968.

Critical Studies

11 ÅHNEBRINK, Lars. *The Beginnings of Naturalism in American Fiction* Cambridge, Mass., 1950.
12 ARVIDSON, F. A., ed. *Centennial Tributes and a Checklist of the Hamlin Garland Papers in the University of Southern California Library.* Los Angeles, 1962.
13 BLEDSOE, T. A., ed. *Main-Travelled Roads: Six Mississippi Valley Stories.* With Introduction. New York, 1954.
14 BROWNE, R. B. "'Popular' & Folk Songs: Unifying Force in Garland's Autobiographical Works." *SFQ*, 25(1961):153–166.
15 CHRISTMAN, H. M., ed. *A Son of the Middle Border.* With Introduction. New York, 1962.
16 DALY, J. P. and S. J. "Hamlin Garland's *Rose of Dutcher's Coolly.*" *ELL*, 11(1962):51–65.

1 EDWARDS, Herbert. "Herne, Garland, and Henry George." *AL*, 28(1956): 359–367.

2 GOLDSTEIN, J. B. "Two Literary Radicals." *AL*, 17(1945):152–160.

3 HIGGINS, J. E. "A Man from the Middle Border: Hamlin Garland's Diaries." *WMH*, 46(1963):294–302.

4 HOWELLS, W. D. "Mr. Garland's Books." *NAR*, 196(1912):523–528.

5 KOERNER, J. D. "Comment on 'Hamlin Garland's Decline from Realism'." *AL*, 26(1954):427–432.

6 LAZENBY, W. "Idealistic Realist on the Platform: Hamlin Garland." *QJS*, 49(1963):138–145.

7 McELDERRY, B. R., Jr., ed. *Boy Life on the Prairie.* With Introduction. Lincoln, Neb., 1961. (Text of first edition, 1899.)

8 MILLER, C. T. "Hamlin Garland's Retreat from Realism." *WAL*, 1(1966):119–129.

9 PIZER, D. "Hamlin Garland's *A Son of the Middle Border:* An Appreciation." *SAQ*, 65(1966):448–459.

10 PIZER, Donald. *Realism and Naturalism in Nineteenth Century American Literature.* Carbondale, Ill., 1966.

11 REAMER, O. J. "Garland and the Indians." *NMQ*, 34(1964):257–280.

12 SCHORER, Mark. "Afterword" to *Main-Travelled Roads.* New York, 1962.†

13 STRONKS, J. B. "Mark Twain's Boston Stage Debut as Seen by Hamlin Garland." *NEQ*, 36(1963):85–86.

14 STRONKS, J. B. "A Realist Experiments with Impressionism; Hamlin Garland's 'Chicago Stories'." *AL*, 36(1964):38–52.

15 WHITFORD, K. "Crusader Without a Cause: An Examination of Hamlin Garland's *Middle Border.*" *MASJ*, 6, i(1965):61–72.

16 WHITFORD, K. "Patterns of Observation: A Study of Hamlin Garland's *Middle Border* Landscape." *TWA*, 50(1961):331–338.

17 WILLIAMS, B. C. *Our Short Story Writers.* New York, 1920.

Nathaniel Hawthorne (1804–1864)

Bibliographies

18 BLAIR, Walter. "Hawthorne." In *Eight American Authors: A Review of Research and Criticism.* New York, 1956. Supplemented by J. C. Mathews in the 1963 printing.

19 BROWNE, Nina Eliza. *A Bibliography of Nathaniel Hawthorne.* Boston, 1905.

20 CATHCART, Wallace H. *Bibliography of the Works of Nathaniel Hawthorne.* Cleveland, 1905.

1 PHILLIPS, Robert S. *"The Scarlet Letter:* A Selected Checklist of Criticism (1850–1962)." *BB*, 22(1962):213–216.

2 PHILLIPS, Robert, Jack KLIGERMAN, Robert E. LONG, and Robert HASTINGS. "Nathaniel Hawthorne: Criticism of the Four Major Romances: A Selected Bibliography." *Thoth*, 3(1962):39–50.

Texts

3 *The Complete Works of Nathaniel Hawthorne, with Introductory Notes.* Ed. by George P. Lathrop. The Riverside Edition. 12 vols. Boston, 1883. (Standard, but being superseded by the Centenary Edition.)

4 *The American Notebooks of Nathaniel Hawthorne.* Ed. by Randall Stewart. New Haven, 1932.

5 *The Complete Novels and Selected Tales of Nathaniel Hawthorne.* Ed. by Norman H. Pearson. New York, 1937. (Includes, beside novels, over thirty tales.)

6 *The English Notebooks of Nathaniel Hawthorne.* Ed. by Randall Stewart. New York, 1941.

7 *Hawthorne as Editor.* Ed. by Arlin Turner. Baton Rouge, 1941. (Reprints Hawthorne's brief essays on a great diversity of topics from *The American Magazine* for 1836.)

8 *The Portable Hawthorne.* Ed. by Malcolm Cowley. New York, 1948. (Includes a dozen tales, and selections from notebooks and letters.)†

9 *The Centenary Edition of the Works of Nathaniel Hawthorne.* Ed. by William Charvat, Roy H. Pearce, C. M. Simpson. Introductions by R. H. Pearce; textual introductions by Fredson Bowers. Columbus, Ohio, 1962– . (In progress. Already published are *The Scarlet Letter, The House of the Seven Gables, The Blithedale Romance, Fanshawe, The Marble Faun.*)

10 (In addition to Hawthorne's novels and notebooks and editorials, he published: *Twice-Told Tales,* 1837; *Grandfather's Chair,* 1841; *Biographical Stories for Children,* 1842; *Twice-Told Tales,* Second Series, 1842; *Mosses from an Old Manse,* 1846; *The Snow Image and Other Twice-Told Tales,* 1851; *The Wonder Book,* 1851; *Tanglewood Tales,* 1853; *Dolliver Romance and Other Pieces,* 1876; *Fanshawe and Other Sketches,* 1876.)

Biographies

11 CANTWELL, Robert. *Nathaniel Hawthorne: The American Years.* New York, 1948.

12 DAVIDSON, Edward H. *Hawthorne's Last Phase.* New Haven, 1949.

13 HAWTHORNE, Julian. *Hawthorne and His Wife.* 2 vols. Boston, 1885. (By his son.)

14 HOELTJE, Hubert H. *Inward Sky: The Mind and Art of Nathaniel Hawthorne.* Durham, N.C., 1962.

15 LATHROP, G. P. *A Study of Hawthorne.* Boston, 1876. (By his son-in-law.)

1   LOGGINS, Vernon. *The Hawthornes: The Story of Seven Generations of an American Family.* New York, 1951.

2   MATHER, Edward. *Nathaniel Hawthorne: A Biography.* New York, 1940.

3   STEWART, Randall. *Nathaniel Hawthorne: A Biography.* New Haven, 1948.

4   WAGENKNECHT, Edward. *Nathaniel Hawthorne: Man and Writer.* New York, 1961.

5   WOODBERRY, George E. *Nathaniel Hawthorne.* Boston, 1902.

Critical Studies

6   ABEL, Darrel. "The Devil in Boston." *PQ*, 32(1953):366–381.

7   ABEL, Darrel. "Hawthorne's Dimmesdale: Fugitive from Wrath." *NCF*, 11(1956):81–105.

8   ABEL, Darrel. "Hawthorne's Hester." *CE*, 13(1952):303–309.

9   ABEL, Darrel. "Hawthorne's Pearl: Symbol and Character." *ELH*, 18(1951):50–66.

10 ABEL, Darrel. "Hawthorne's Skepticism About Social Reform with Especial Reference to *The Blithedale Romance.*" *UKCR*, 19(1953):181–193.

11 ARVIN, Newton. *Hawthorne.* Boston, 1929.

12 BAYM, Nina. "The Head, the Heart, and the Unpardonable Sin." *NEQ*, 40(1967):31–47.

13 BELL, Millicent. *Hawthorne's View of the Artist.* New York, 1962.

14 BEWLEY, Marius. "Hawthorne's Novels." In *The Eccentric Design: Form in the Classic American Novel.* London, 1959.

15 BEWLEY, Marius. "James's Debt to Hawthorne (I): *The Blithedale Romance* and *The Bostonians.*" *Scrutiny*, 16(1949):301–317.

16 BEWLEY, Marius. "James's Debt to Hawthorne (II): *The Marble Faun* and *The Wings of the Dove.*" *Scrutiny*, 16(1949):301–317.

17 BIER, Jesse. "Hawthorne on the Romance: His Prefaces Related and Examined." *MP*, 53(1955):17–24.

18 BIRDSALL, Virginia Ogden. "Hawthorne's Fair-Haired Maidens: The Fading Light." *PMLA*, 75(1960):250–256.

19 BLAIR, Walter. "Color, Light, and Shadow in Hawthorne's Fiction." *NEQ*, 15(1942):74–94.

20 BRADLEY, Sculley, R. C. BEATTY, and E. H. LONG, eds. *The Scarlet Letter: An Annotated Text, Backgrounds and Sources, Essays in Criticism.* New York, 1962. (Essays by various hands.)†

21 BRODTKORB, Paul, Jr. "Art Allegory in *The Marble Faun,*" *PMLA*, 77(1962):254–267.

22 BROWNELL, William C. *American Prose Masters.* New York, 1909.†

23 CARLETON, William G. "Hawthorne Discovers the English." *YR*, 53(1964):395–414.

1 CARPENTER, Frederic I. "Puritans Preferred Blondes: The Heroines of Melville and Hawthorne." *NEQ*, 9(1936):253–272.

2 CARPENTER, Frederic I. "Scarlet A. Minus." *CE*, 5(1944):173–180. Repr. in Carpenter's *American Literature and the Dream*. New York, 1955.

3 CARPENTER, Richard C. "Hawthorne's Polar Explorations: 'Young Goodman Brown' and 'My Kinsman, Major Molineax'." *NCF*, 24(1969): 45–56.

4 CHANDLER, Elizabeth L. *A Study of the Sources of the Tales and Romances. Written by Nathaniel Hawthorne before 1853.* Northampton, Mass., 1926.

5 CHARNEY, Maurice. "Hawthorne and the Gothic Style." *NEQ*, 34(1961): 36–49.

6 CLARK, Harry H. "Hawthorne: Tradition *versus* Innovation." In *Patterns of Commitment in American Literature*. Ed. by Marston LaFrance. Toronto, 1967.

7 CLARK, Harry H. "Hawthorne's Literary and Aesthetic Doctrines as Embodied in his Tales." *TWA*, 50(1961):251–275.

8 COHEN, B. Bernard, ed. *The Recognition of Nathaniel Hawthorne: Selected Criticism Since 1828.* Ann Arbor, Mich., 1969.

9 COWLEY, Malcolm. "Five Acts of *The Scarlet Letter*." *CE*, 19(1957):11–16.

10 COWLEY, Malcolm. "Hawthorne in the Looking-Glass." *SR*, 56(1948): 545–563.

11 CRONIN, M. "Hawthorne on Romantic Love and the Status of Woman." *PMLA*, 69(1954):89–98.

12 DAVIDSON, Edward H. "Hawthorne and the Pathetic Fallacy." *JEGP*, 54(1955):486–497.

13 DAVIDSON, Frank. "Thoreau's Contributions to Hawthorne's *Mosses*." *NEQ*, 20(1947):532–542.

14 DONAHUE, Agnes M., ed. *A Casebook on the Hawthorne Question*. New York, 1963.

15 DOUBLEDAY, Neal F. "Hawthorne's Hester and Feminism." *PMLA*, 54(1949):825–828.

16 DURR, Robert Allen. "Hawthorne's Ironic Mode." *NEQ*, 30(1957): 486–495.

17 EISINGER, C. E. "Hawthorne as Champion of the Middle Way." *NEQ*, 27(1954):27–52. (Limited to his short stories.)

18 FICK, Leonard J. *The Light Beyond: A Study of Hawthorne's Theology.* Westminster, Md., 1955.

19 FOGLE, Richard Harter. *Hawthorne's Fiction: The Light and the Dark.* Norman, Okla., 1952.

20 FOGLE, Richard Harter. *Hawthorne's Imagery: The "Proper Light and Shadow" in the Major Romances.* Norman, Okla., 1969.

21 FOLSOM, James K. *Man's Accidents and God's Purposes: Multiplicity in Hawthorne's Fiction.* New Haven, 1963.†

22 FOSTER, C. H. "Hawthorne's Literary Theory." *PMLA*, 57(1942):241–255.

1 FUSSELL, Edwin. *Frontier: American Literature and the American West.* Princeton, 1965. (Includes Hawthorne's attitude toward the forest and nature.)

2 GROSS, Seymour L. "Hawthorne Versus Melville." *BuR*, 14(1966):89–109.

3 GROSS, Seymour L., ed. *A "Scarlet Letter" Handbook.* San Francisco, 1960. (Essays by various hands; excellent bibliography.)†

4 GUPTA, R. H. "Hawthorne's Theory of Art." *AL*, 40(1968):309–324.

5 HALL, Lawrence Sargent. *Hawthorne, Critic of Society.* New Haven, 1944.

6 "Hawthorne Centenary Issue." *NCF*, 19(1964). (Articles by diverse critics.)

7 JAMES, Henry. *Hawthorne.* London, 1879.†

8 JONES, Buford. "'The Hall of Fantasy' and the Early Hawthorne-Thoreau Relationship." *PMLA*, 83(1968):1429–1438.

9 KESSELRING, Marion Louise. *Hawthorne's Reading, 1828–1850.* New York, 1949.

10 KIMBROUGH, Robert. "The Actual and the Imaginary: Hawthorne's Concept of Art in Theory and Practice." *TWA*, 50(1961):277–293.

11 LASSER, Marvin. "'Head,' 'Heart,' and 'Will' in Hawthorne's Psychology." *NCF*, 10(1955):130–140.

12 LEVIN, Harry. *The Power of Blackness: Hawthorne, Poe, Melville.* New York, 1958.†

13 LUNDBLAD, Jane. *Hawthorne and the Tradition of Gothic Romance.* Cambridge, Mass., 1946.

14 LUNDBLAD, Jane. *Nathaniel Hawthorne and European Literary Tradition.* Cambridge, Mass., 1947.

15 MALE, Roy R. *Hawthorne's Tragic Vision.* Austin, Tex., 1957.†

16 MARTIN, Terence J. *Nathaniel Hawthorne.* New York, 1965.†

17 MATTHIESSEN, F. O. *American Renaissance.* New York, 1941.†

18 McPHERSON, Hugo. *Hawthorne as Myth-Maker: A Study in Imagination.* Toronto, 1969.

19 MILLS, Barriss. "Hawthorne and Puritanism." *NEQ*, 21(1948):78–102.

20 MORE, Paul E. "The Solitude of Nathaniel Hawthorne." *AtlM*, 88(1901):588–599.

21 PEARCE, Roy Harvey, ed. *Hawthorne Centenary Essays.* Columbus, Ohio, 1964. (Essays by diverse critics.)

22 RINGE, Donald. "Hawthorne's Psychology of the Head and Heart," *PMLA*, 65(1950):120–132.

23 SCHUBERT, Leland. *Hawthorne, the Artist: Fine-Art Devices in Fiction.* Chapel Hill, 1944.

24 SCHWARTZ, Joseph. "Three Aspects of Hawthorne's Puritanism." *NEQ*, 36(1963):192–208.

1   STEIN, W. B. *Hawthorne's Faust: A Study of the Devil Archetype.* Gainesville, Fla., 1953.

2   STEWART, Randall. "Hawthorne and the Civil War." *SP*, 34(1937):91–106.

3   STEWART, Randall. "Hawthorne and the Faerie Queene." *PQ*, 12(1933): 196–206.

4   STEWART, Randall. "Melville and Hawthorne." *SAQ*, 51(1952):436–466.

5   STUBBS, John C. "Hawthorne's *The Scarlet Letter:* The Theory of The Romance and the Use of the New England Situation." *PMLA*, 83(1968): 1439–1447. (To be expanded as a book shortly.)

6   TURNER, Arlin. "Hawthorne and Reform." *NEQ*, 15(1942):700–714.

7   TURNER, Arlin. "Hawthorne as Self-Critic." *SAQ*, 37(1938):132–138.

8   TURNER, Arlin. "Hawthorne's Literary Borrowings." *PMLA* 51(1936): 542–562.

9   TURNER, Arlin. *Nathaniel Hawthorne: An Introduction and Interpretation.* New York, 1961.†

10   VAN DOREN, Mark. *Nathaniel Hawthorne: A Critical Biography.* New York, 1949.†

11   WAGGONER, Hyatt H. *Hawthorne: A Critical Study.* Cambridge, Mass., 1955. Rev. ed., 1963, with a chapter added on *Marble Faun.*

12   WAGGONER, Hyatt H. *Nathaniel Hawthorne.* Minneapolis, 1962.†

13   WARREN, Austin. "Introduction" to *Hawthorne: Representative Selections.* New York, 1934.

Oliver Wendell Holmes (1809–1894)

Bibliography

14   CURRIER, T. F. *A Bibliography of Oliver Wendell Holmes.* Ed. by Eleanor M. Tilton. New York, 1953.

Texts

15   *Complete Poetical Works of Oliver Wendell Holmes.* Ed. by H. E. Scudder. Boston, 1895.

16   *The Writings of Oliver Wendell Holmes.* Boston, 1904. (Earlier edition [1891] does not include *Emerson* and *Motley.*)

17   *The Autocrat's Miscellanies.* Ed. with Introduction by A. Mordell. New York, 1959. (Prints 30 uncollected essays.)

Biographies

18   MORSE, J. T. *Life and Letters of Oliver Wendell Holmes.* 2 vols. Boston, 1896.

1 TILTON, Eleanor M. *The Amiable Autocrat: A Biography of Dr. Oliver Wendell Holmes.* New York, 1947.

Critical Studies

2 ADKINS, Nelson. "'The Chambered Nautilus': Its Scientific and Poetic Backgrounds." *AL*, 9(1938):458–465.

3 ALLEN, G. W. *American Prosody.* New York, 1935.

4 ARMS, George. "Holmes." In *The Fields Were Green.* Stanford, Calif., 1953.

5 BOEWE, C. "Reflex Action in the Novels of Oliver Wendell Holmes." *AL*, 26(1954):303–319.

6 BROM, H. Introduction to *The Autocrat.* . . . New York, 1957.

7 CLARK, Harry H. "Dr. Holmes: A Reinterpretation." *NEQ*, 12(1939): 19–34.

8 CONNER, F. W. *Cosmic Optimism: A Study of the Interpretation of Evolution by American Poets from Emerson to Robinson.* Gainesville, Fla., 1949.

9 CURRIER, Thomas F. "Oliver Wendell Holmes, Poet Laureate of Harvard." *PMHS*, 67(1945):436–451.

10 EBY, Cecil D., Jr. "The 'Lesson' in 'The Chambered Nautilus'." *ESQ*, 27(1962):48–50.

11 FIELDS, A. *Authors and Friends.* Boston, 1898.

12 FULLER, H. D. "Holmes." In *American Writers on American Literature.* Ed. by John Macy. New York, 1931.

13 HAYAKAWA, S. I. "The Boston Poet Laureate: Oliver Wendell Holmes." *TexSE*, 16(1936):572–592.

14 HAYAKAWA, S. I., and Howard M. JONES, eds. *Oliver Wendell Holmes: Representative Selections, with Introduction, Bibliography and Notes.* New York, 1939. (Has documented Introduction of over 100 pp.)

15 HOWE, M. A. DeW. *Holmes of the Breakfast Table.* New York, 1939.

16 JONES, Howard M. "Oliver Wendell Holmes, 1890–1894." In *History and the Contemporary.* Madison, 1964.

17 KERN, A. C. "Dr. Oliver Wendell Holmes Today." *UKCR*, 14(1948): 191–199.

18 KNICKERBOCKER, W. S. "His Own Boswell: A Note on the Poetry of Oliver Wendell Holmes." *SR*, 41(1933):454–466.

19 MATTHEWS, Brander "Holmes." In *Cambridge History of American Literature.* New York, 1918.

20 MATTSON, J. Stanley. "Oliver Wendell Holmes and *The Deacon's Masterpiece:* A Logical Story?" *NEQ*, 41(1968):104–114.

21 OBERNDORF, C. P. *The Psychiatric Novels of Oliver Wendell Holmes.* New York, 1943.

22 PEARCE, R. H. *The Continuity of American Poetry.* Princeton, 1961.†

1 PRITCHARD, J. P. "The Autocrat and Horace." *CW*, 25(1932):217–223.
2 QUINN, A. H., ed. *The Literature of the American People*. New York, 1951. ("The Rationalist in Literature".)
3 SMALL, M. R., ed. *Elsie Venner*. New York, 1961. (With "Afterword.")
4 SMALL, Miriam R. *Oliver Wendell Holmes*. New York, 1962.†
5 STEPHEN, L. *Studies of a Biographer*. London, 1907.
6 TILTON, Eleanor M. "Holmes and His Critic Motley." *AL*, 36(1965): 463–474.
7 WAGGONER, Hyatt H. *American Poets*. Boston, 1968.
8 WEBB, Howard. "Holmes' 'The Deacon's Masterpiece'." *Expl*, 24(1965):17.
9 WESTERSDORF, K. P. "The Underground Workshop of Oliver Wendell Holmes." *AL*, 35(1963):1–12.
10 WOOLF, V. "Oliver Wendell Holmes." In *Granite and Rainbow: Essays*. London, 1958.
11 YNDURAIN, F. "Afinidades Electivas: Unamicno y Holmes." *RJ*, 15(1964):335–354.

William Dean Howells (1837–1920)

Bibliographies

12 GIBSON, W. M., and George ARMS. *A Bibliography of William Dean Howells*. New York, 1948. First published in *BNYPL*, 51(1946–47).
13 LYDENBERG, John, and Edwin CADY. "The Howells Revival: Rounds Two and Three." *NEQ*, 32(1959):394–407.
14 WOODRESS, James, and S. P. ANDERSON, compilers. "A Bibliography of Writings about W. D. Howells," in *American Literary Realism, 1870–1910*. Special Number 1969. Pp. 1–133.

Texts

15 Beyond Howells's novels, the following are especially noteworthy: *Venetian Life*, 1866; *Italian Journeys*, 1867; *Three Villages*, 1884; *Tuscan Cities*, 1885; *Modern Italian Poets*, 1887; *Criticism and Fiction* [from "Editor's Study"], 1892; *A Little Swiss Sojourn*, 1892; *My Literary Passions*, 1895; *Impressions and Experiences*, 1896; *Literary Friends and Acquaintance*, 1900; *Heroines of Fiction*, 1901; *Literature and Life*, 1902; *London Films*, 1905; *Certain Delightful English Towns*, 1906; *Roman Holidays*, 1908; *Seven English Cities*, 1909; *Imaginary Interviews* [from "Easy Chair"], 1910; *My Mark Twain*, 1910; *Familiar Spanish Travels*, 1913; *Great Modern American Stories*, 1920; *Hither and Thither in Germany*, 1920.

1 *The Writings of William Dean Howells.* Library Edition. 6 vols. New York, 1911. (*My Literary Passions* and *Criticism and Fiction, The Landlord at Lion's Head, Literature and Life, London Films* and *Certain Delightful English Towns, Literary Friends and Acquaintance* [with *My Mark Twain*], *A Hazard of New Fortunes.*) (Will be superseded by a complete edition in progress at Indiana University.)

2 *Life in Letters of William Dean Howells.* Ed. by Mildred Howells. 2 vols. Garden City, New York, 1928.

3 *William Dean Howells: Representative Selections, with Introduction, Bibliography, and Notes.* Ed. by Clara and Rudolf Kirk. New York, 1950.†

4 "The Lowell-Howells Friendship: Some Unpublished Letters." Ed. by James Woodress. *NEQ,* 26(1953):523–528.

5 *Preface to Contemporaries, 1882–1920.* Ed. with an Introduction and Bibliographical Note by George Arms, William Gibson, and F. C. Marston, Jr. Gainesville, Fla., 1957.

6 *A Traveler from Altruria.* Ed. by H. M. Jones. New York, 1957.†

7 *Criticism and Fiction and Other Essays.* Ed. by Rudolf and Clara Kirk. New York, 1959.

8 *Life of Abraham Lincoln.* Ed. by C. C. Walton. Bloomington, Ind., 1960.

9 *Mark Twain-Howells Letters: The Correspondence of Samuel L. Clemens and William D. Howells, 1872–1910.* Ed. by H. N. Smith and William M. Gibson. 2 vols. Cambridge, Mass., 1960.

10 KIRK, Clara and Rudolf. *Letters of An Altrurian Traveler (1893–1894).* A Facsimile Reproduction with an Introduction by Clara and Rudolf Kirk. Gainesville, Fla., 1961.

11 *A Selected Edition of W. D. Howells.* Ed. by Edwin H. Cady, Ronald Gottesman, et al. Bloomington, Ind., 1968– . Thus far published are *Their Wedding Journey* (ed. by John K. Reeves) and *Literary Friends and Acquaintance* (ed. by David F. Hiatt and Edwin H. Cady). 30 vols.

Biography

12 BENNETT, George. *William Dean Howells: The Development of a Novelist.* Norman, Okla., 1959.

13 BROOKS, Van Wyck. *Howells: His Life and World.* New York, 1959.

14 CADY, Edwin H. *The Realist at War: The Mature Years, 1885–1920, of William Dean Howells.* Syracuse, N.Y., 1958.

15 CADY, Edwin H. *The Road to Realism. The Early Years, 1837–1885, of William Dean Howells.* Syracuse, N.Y., 1956.

16 CARRINGTON, George C. *The Immense Complex Drama: The World and Art of the Howells Novel.* Columbus, Ohio, 1966. (Included for data beyond the novel *qua* novel.)

1 CARTER, Everett. *Howells and the Age of Realism.* Philadelphia, 1954.

2 COOKE, D. G. *William Dean Howells: A Critical Study.* New York, 1922.

3 FIRKINS, O. W. *William Dean Howells: A Study.* Cambridge, Mass., 1924.

4 FRYCKSTEDT, O. W. *In Quest of America: A Study of Howells' Early Development as a Novelist.* Uppsala, 1958; Cambridge, Mass., 1959.

5 HOUGH, R. L. *The Quiet Rebel: William Dean Howells as Social Commentator.* Lincoln, Neb., 1959.

6 KANE, Patricia. "Mutual Perspective: James and Howells as Critics of Each Other's Fiction." *MinnR,* 7(1967):331–341.

7 KIRK, Clara. *Howells and the Art in His Time.* New Brunswick, N.J., 1965.

8 KIRK, Clara. *W. D. Howells: Traveler from Altruria.* New Brunswick, N.J., 1962.

9 KIRK, Clara and Rudolph. "Introduction" to *Howells: Representative Selections.* New York, 1950.

10 KIRK, Clara and Rudolf. *William Dean Howells.* New York, 1962.

11 VANDERBILT, Kermit. *The Achievement of William Dean Howells: A Reinterpretation.* Princeton, 1968.

12 WILLIAMS, S. T. *The Spanish Background of American Literature.* 2 vols. New Haven, 1955.

13 WOODRESS, James L. *Howells and Italy.* Durham, N.C., 1952.

14 WRIGHT, Nathalia. *American Novelists in Italy.* Philadelphia, 1965.

Critical Studies

15 ÅHNEBRINK, Lars. *The Beginnings of Naturalism in American Fiction.* Cambridge, Mass., 1950.

16 ANICETTI, Luigi. "William Dean Howells, Console a Venezia (1861–1865)." *NRS,* 41(1957):87–106.

17 ARMS, George. "Further Inquiry into Howells's Socialism." *S&S,* 3(1939):245–248.

18 ARMS, George. "Howells' English Travel Books: Problems in Technique." *PMLA,* 82(1967):104–116.

19 ARMS, George. "The Literary Background of Howells's Social Criticism." *AL,* 14(1942):260–276.

20 BEACH, J. W. "An American Master." *YR,* n.s. 15(1926):399–401. (Reviews of Firkins' *Howells* and Phelps' *Howells, James, Bryant.*)

21 BEACH, J. W. Review of Cooke's *Howells. JEGP,* 22(1923):451–454.

1 BELCHER, H. G. "Howells's Opinions on the Religious Conflicts of His Age as Exhibited in Magazine Articles." *AL*, 15(1943):262–278.

2 BERTHOFF, Warner. *The Ferment of Realism: American Literature 1884–1919.* New York, 1965.

3 BETTS, W. W., Jr. "The Relations of William Dean Howells to German Life and Letters." In *Anglo-German and American-German Crosscurrents.* Chapel Hill, N.C., 1957.

4 BOARDMAN, Arthur. "Social Point of View in the Novels of William Dean Howells." *AL*, 39(1967):42–59.

5 BUDD, L. J. "Altruism Arrives in America." *AQ*, 8(1956):40–52.

6 BUDD, L. J. "Howells, the *Atlantic Monthly*, and Republicanism." *AL*, 24(1952):139–156.

7 BUDD, L. J. "Howells' 'Blistering and Cauterizing'." *OSAHQ*, 62(1953): 334–347.

8 BUDD, L. J. "Twain, Howells, and the Boston Nihilists." *NEQ*, 32(1959): 351–371.

9 BUDD, L. J. "William Dean Howells' Debt to Tolstoy." *ASEER*, 9(1950): 292–301.

10 BUDD, L. J. "W. D. Howells' Defense of the Romance." *PMLA*, 67(1952): 32–42.

11 CADY, E. H. "Armando Palacio Valdes Writes to William Dean Howells." *Symposium*, 2(1948):19–37.

12 CADY, E. H. "The Gentleman as Socialist: William Dean Howells," in *The Gentleman in America.* Syracuse, N.Y., 1949.

13 CADY, E. H. "Howells in 1948." *UKCR*, 15(1948):83–91.

14 CADY, E. H. "The Neuroticism of William Dean Howells." *PMLA*, 61(1946):229–238.

15 CADY, E. H. "A Note on Howells and 'the Smiling Aspects of Life'." *AL*, 17(1945):175–178.

16 CADY, E. H. "William Dean Howells and the Ashtabula *Sentinel*." *OSAHQ*, 53(1944):39–51.

17 CADY, E. H. "William Dean Howells in Italy: Some Bibliographical Notes." *Symposium*, 7(1953):147–153.

18 CADY, Edwin H., and David L. FRAZIER, eds. *The War of the Critics over William Dean Howells.* Evanston, Ill., 1962. (A collection of critical essays, mainly by Howells' contemporaries. Includes Woodress' summary-survey.)

19 CARGILL, Oscar. "Henry James's 'Moral Policeman': William Dean Howells." *AL*, 29(1958):371–398.

20 CARTER, Everett. "The Haymarket Affair in Literature." *AQ*, 2(1950): 270–278.

21 CARTER, Everett. "William Dean Howells' Theory of Critical Realism." *ELH*, 16(1949):151–166.

22 CARTER, P. J., Jr. "The Influence of William Dean Howells upon Mark Twain's Social Satire." *UCSLL*, 4(1953):93–100.

1 CLARK, H. H. "The Role of Science in the Thought of W. D. Howells."
TWA, 42(1953):263–303.

2 CLEMENS, S. L. "William Dean Howells." *Harper's*, 113(1906):221–225.
Repr. in *What is Man? and Other Essays*. New York, 1917.

3 CRONKHITE, G. F. "Howells Turns to the Inner Life." *NEQ*, 30(1957):
474–485.

4 DeMILLE, G. E. "The Infallible Dean." *SR*, 36(1928):148–156. Repr.
in *Literary Criticism in America*. New York, 1931.

5 DOVE, J. R. "Howells' Irrational Heroines." *TexSE*, 35(1956):64–80.

6 DOWLING, J. A. "W. D. Howells' Literary Reputation in England, 1882–
1897." *DR*, 45(1965):277–288.

7 EBLE, K. E. "The Western Ideals of William Dean Howells." *WHR*,
11(1957):331–338.

8 EBLE, K. E., ed. *Howells: A Century of Criticism*. Dallas, Tex., 1962.
(Reprints essays by various critics chronologically arranged.)

9 EDWARDS, Herbert. "Howells and the Controversy over Realism in
American Fiction." *AL*, 3(1931):237–248.

10 EDWARDS, Herbert. "Howells and Herne." *AL*, 22(1951):432–441.

11 EKSTROM, Kjell. "The Cable-Howells Correspondence." *SN*, 22(1950):
48–61.

12 EKSTROM, W. F. "Equalitarian Principle in the Fiction of W. D. Howells."
AL, 24(1952):40–50.

13 ELKINS, K. C. "Eliot, Howells, and the Courses of Graduate Instruction,
1869–1871." *HLB*, 10(1956):141–146.

14 FALK, Robert P. "The Literary Criticism of the Genteel Decades, 1870–
1900." In *The Development of American Literary Criticism*. Ed. by F. Stovall.
Chapel Hill, N.C., 1955.†

15 FALK, Robert P. *The Victorian Mode in American Fiction, 1865–1885*.
East Lansing, Mich., 1965.

16 FOSTER, Richard. "The Contemporaneity of Howells." *NEQ*, 32(1959):
54–78.

17 FOX, A. B. "Howells as a Religious Critic." *NEQ*, 25(1952):199–216.

18 FOX, A. B. "Howells' Doctrine of Complicity." *MLQ*, 13(1952):56–60.

19 FREE, W. J. "Howells' 'Editha' and Pragmatic Belief." *SSF*, 3(1966):
285–292.

20 FRYCKSTEDT, O. W. "Howells and Conway in Venice." *SN*, 30(1958):
165–174.

21 GARLAND, Hamlin. "Howells." In *American Writers on American
Literature*. Ed. by John Macy. New York, 1931.

22 GARLAND, Hamlin. "Roadside Meetings of a Literary Nomad, II:
William Dean Howells and Other Memories of Boston." *Bookman*,
70(1929):246–250. Repr. in *Roadside Meetings*. New York, 1930.

1 GETTMAN, R. A. "Turgenev in England and America." *UISLL*, 27(1941): 51–63.

2 GETZELS, J. W. "William Dean Howells and Socialism." *S&S*, 2(1938): 376–386.

3 GIBSON, William M. "Mark Twain and Howells, Anti-Imperialists." *NEQ*, 20(1947):435–470.

4 GIBSON, William M. *William Dean Howells.* Minneapolis, 1967.†

5 GOHDES, Clarence. *The Literature of the American People.* Ed. by A. H. Quinn. New York, 1951.

6 GOLDFARB, Clare R. "From Complicity to Altruria: The Use of Tolstoi in Howells." *UKCR*, 32(1966):311–317.

7 GORLIER, Claudio. "William Dean Howells e le definizioni del realismo." *SA*, 2(1956):83–125.

8 GULLASON, T. A. "New Light on the Crane-Howells Relationship." *NEQ*, 20(1957):389–392.

9 HAIGHT, G. S. "Realism Defined: William Dean Howells." In *Literary History of the United States.* Ed. by Robert E. Spiller, et al. New York, 1948.

10 HARLOW, Virginia. "William Dean Howells and Thomas Sergeant Perry." *BPLQ*, 1(1949):135–150.

11 JAMES, Henry. "A Letter to Mr. Howells." *NAR*, 195(1912):558–562.

12 JAMES, Henry. "William Dean Howells." *HW*, 30(June 19, 1886):394–395.

13 KIRK, Clara M. "Reality and Actuality in the March Family Narratives of W. D. Howells." *PMLA*, 74(1959):137–152.

14 KIRK, Clara and Rudolf. "Howells and the Church of the Carpenter." *NEQ*, 32(1959):185–206.

15 [LOWELL, J. R.] Review of *Venetian Life. NAR*, 103(1866):610–613. Repr. in Lowell's *The Function of the Poet.* Ed. by Albert Mordell. Boston, 1920.

16 LUTWACK, Leonard. "William Dean Howells and the 'Editor's Study'." *AL*, 24(1952):195–207. See also Jay Martin.

17 MATTHEWS, Brander. "Mr. Howells as a Critic." *Forum*, 32(1902): 629–638.

18 MESERVE, W. J. "Truth, Morality, and Swedenborg in Howells' Theory of Realism." *NEQ*, 27(1954):252–257.

19 MILLER, F. DeW. "Identification of Contributors to the *North American Review* under Lowell." *SB*, 6(1954):225. (Reviews of Howells' books, 1866–1872.)

20 MOFFITT, Cecil L. "William Dean Howells and the South." *MissQ*, 20(1967):13–24.

21 MORBY, E. S. "William Dean Howells and Spain." *HR*, 14(1946):187–212.

22 MORGAN, H. Wayne. *American Writers in Rebellion from Mark Twain to Dreiser.* New York, 1965.†

50   MAJOR AMERICAN WRITERS

1 MUNFORD, H. M. "The Disciple Proves Independent: Howells and Lowell." *PMLA*, 74(1959):484–487.

2 MURRAY, D. M. "Henry B. Fuller: Friend of Howells." *SAQ*, 52(1953): 431–444.

3 NOBLE, David W. "W. D. Howells: The Discovery of Society." *MQ*, 3(1962):149–162.

4 PARKS, E. W. "Howells and the Gentle Reader." *SAQ*, 50(1951):239–247.

5 PARKS, E. W. "A Realist Avoids Reality: W. D. Howells and the Civil War Years." *SAQ*, 52(1953):93–97.

6 PARRINGTON, V. L. "William Dean Howells and the Realism of the Commonplace." In *Main Currents in American Thought*. New York, 1930.†

7 PAYNE, Alma J. "The Family in the Utopia of William Dean Howells." *GaR*, 15(1961):217–229.

8 PEARCE, R. H. "Adams, Howells, and Their Advocates." *VQR*, 35(1959): 149–153. (Review article on Cady's biography.)

9 [PERRY, T. S.] "William Dean Howells." *Century*, 23(1882):680–685.

10 PIZER, Donald. "The Evolutionary Foundation of W. D. Howells's *Criticism and Fiction*." *PQ*, 40(1961):91–103.

11 PIZER, Donald. "Evolutionary Literary Criticism and the Defense of Howellsian Realism." *JEGP*, 61(1962):296–304.

12 PRITCHARD, J. P. "William Dean Howells." In *Return to the Fountains*. Durham, N.C., 1942.

13 PRITCHARD, John Paul. *Criticism in America*. Norman, Okla., 1956.

14 QUINN, A. H. "William Dean Howells and the Establishment of Realism." In *American Fiction*. New York, 1936.

15 RATNER, Marc L. "Howells and Boyesen: Two Views of Realism." *NEQ*, 35(1962):376–390.

16 SMITH, Bernard. "Democracy and Realism, III." In *Forces in American Criticism*. New York, 1939.

17 SOKOLOFF, B. A. "William Dean Howells and the Ohio Village: A Study of Environment and Art." *AQ*, 11(1959):58–75.

18 TAYLOR, W. G. "William Dean Howells." In *The Economic Novel in America*. Chapel Hill, N.C., 1942.

19 TRILLING, Lionel. "W. D. Howells and the Roots of Modern Taste." *PR*, 18(1951):516–513. Repr. in *The Opposing Self: Nine Essays in Criticism*. New York, 1955.†

20 WESTBROOK, Max. "The Critical Implications of Howells' Realism." *TexSE*, 36(1957):71–79.

21 WRIGHT, Conrad. "The Sources of Mr. Howells's Socialism." *S&S*, 2(1938):514–517.

Henry James (1843–1916)

Bibliographies

1   BEEBE, Maurice, and W. T. STAFFORD, "Criticism of Henry James: A Selected Checklist with an Index to Studies of Separate Works." *MFS*, 3(1957):73–96.

2   EDEL, Leon, and D. H. LAURENCE. *A Bibliography of Henry James.* London, 1959; rev., 1961. (Supersedes several earlier bibliographies.)†

3   SPILLER, Robert E. "James." In *Eight American Authors.* Ed. by Floyd Stovall. Supplemented by J. C. Mathews in 1963 repr.†

4   STAFFORD, W. T. "Criticism of Henry James: A Selected Checklist." *MFS*, 12(1966):117–177.

Texts (*Other than Novels and Dramas*)

5   *French Poets and Novelists.* London, 1878†

6   *Hawthorne.* London, 1879.†

7   *Portraits of Places.* London, 1883.

8   *A Little Tour of France.* Boston, 1885.

9   *Partial Portraits.* London, 1888. (Includes "The Art of Fiction," 1885.)

10   *Essays in London and Elsewhere.* New York, 1893.

11   *William Wetmore Story and His Friends.* 2 vols. Edinburgh, 1903.

12   *English Hours.* Boston, 1905.

13   *The Question of Our Speech. The Lesson of Balzac.* Boston, 1905.

14   *The American Scene.* New York, 1907.†

15   Prefaces in *The Novels and Tales of Henry James.* The New York Edition. New York, 1907–1917.

16   *Italian Hours.* Boston, 1909.

17   *A Small Boy and Others.* New York, 1913.†

18   *Notes on Novelists, with Some Other Notes.* New York, 1914.

19   *England at War: An Essay.* London, 1915.

20   *The Middle Years.* New York, 1917.

21   *Within the Rim and Other Essays, 1914–1915.* London, 1918.

22   *Notes and Reviews.* Cambridge, Mass., 1921.

23   *The Art of the Novel.* Ed. by R. P. Blackmur. New York, 1934. (Reprints James's prefaces to the New York Edition of his fiction, with an incisive Introduction.)†

1   *Henry James: Representative Selections, with Introduction, Bibliography, and Notes.* Ed. by Lyon Richardson. New York, 1941; rev., 1966.†

2   *The Notebooks of Henry James.* Ed. by F. O. Matthiessen and Kenneth Murdock. New York, 1947.†

3   *The American Essays.* Ed. with Introduction by Leon Edel. New York, 1956.†

4   *The Future of the Novel: Essays on the Art of Fiction.* Ed. with Introduction by Leon Edel. New York, 1956.†

5   *The House of Fiction: Essays on the Novel.* Ed. by Leon Edel. London, 1957.†

6   *Parisian Sketches: Letters to the New York Tribune, 1875–1876.* Ed. by Leon Edel and Ilse D. Lind. New York, 1957.

7   *The Art of Travel.* Ed. by Morton D. Zabel. Garden City, N.Y., 1958. (Selections from James' several books on travels, with introduction.)

8   *Henry James and H. G. Wells: A Record of Their Friendship, Their Debate on the Art of Fiction, and Their Quarrel.* Ed. with Introduction by Leon Edel and Gordon N. Ray. Urbana, Ill., 1958.

9   "Henry James and the *Bazar* Letters." Ed. by Leon Edel and Lyall Powers. *BNYPL*, 62(1958):75–103. (Thirty letters by James to editor of *Harper's Bazar*.)

10   *The Complete Tales of Henry James.* Ed. by Leon Edel. 12 vols. Philadelphia, 1961–1964. (Includes 112 short stories.)

Biographies

11   ANDERSON, Quentin. *The American Henry James.* New Brunswick, N.J., 1957. (Emphasizes influence of James's father's Swedenborgianism.)

12   BELL, Millicent. *Edith Wharton and Henry James: The Story of Their Friendship.* New York, 1965.

13   BOWDEN, Edwin T. *The Themes of Henry James: A System of Observation through the Visual Arts.* New Haven, 1956.

14   BROOKS, Van Wyck. *The Pilgrimage of Henry James.* New York, 1925. (Emphasizes deracination.)

15   DUPEE, F. W. *Henry James.* New York, 1951.†

16   EDEL, Leon. *Henry James: The Untried Years, 1843–1870.* Philadelphia, 1953. *The Conquest of London, 1870–1881; The Middle Years, 1882–1895.* Philadelphia, 1962. *The Treacherous Years, 1895–1905.* 1969. Definitive biography.)†

17   HARLOW, Virginia. *Thomas Sargeant Perry.* Durham, N.C., 1950. (Includes about 100 letters by Henry James.)

18   LEBOWITZ, Naomi. *The Imagination of Loving.* Detroit, 1965.

19   McELDERRY, B. R. *Henry James.* New York, 1965.

20   WHARTON, Edith. *A Backward Glance.* New York, 1934.

Critical Studies

1 BARRETT, Lawrence. "Young Henry James, Critic." *AL*, 20(1949): 508–521.

2 BEACH, J. W. *The Method of Henry James*. New Haven, 1918; rev., 1956.

3 BEWLEY, Marius. "James's Debt to Hawthorne." *Scrutiny*, 16(1949): 178–195, 301–317; 17(1950):14–37. Repr. in Bewley's *The Complex Fate*. London, 1952.

4 BONTLY, Thomas J. "The Aesthetics of Discretion: Sexuality in the Fiction of Henry James." *DA*, 27(1967):3446A–47A (Stanford).

5 BOOTH, Bradford A. "Henry James and the Economic Motif." *NCF*, 8(1953):141–150.

6 BROWNELL, W. C. "James." In *American Prose Masters*. New York, 1909.†

7 BUITENHUIS, Peter. "Henry James on Hawthorne." *NEQ*, 32(1959): 207–225.

8 CANBY, Henry S. *Turn West, Turn East: Mark Twain and Henry James*. Boston, 1951.

9 CARGILL, Oscar. "Henry James's 'Moral Policeman': William Dean Howells." *AL*, 29(1958):371–398.

10 CARGILL, Oscar. *The Novels of Henry James*. New York, 1961. (Cites from a mass of interpretative studies which go beyond the novel *qua* novel.)

11 CLARK, Harry H. "Henry James and Science: *The Wings of the Dove*." *TWA*, 52(1963):1–15.

12 CREWS, Frederick. *The Tragedy of Manners: Moral Drama in the Late Novels of Henry James*. New Haven, 1957.

13 DAICHES, David. "Sensibility and Technique: Preface to a Critique of Henry James." *KR*, 5(1943):569–579.

14 DUPEE, Frederick, ed. *The Question of Henry James*. New York, 1945. (A collection of 25 essays by diverse hands.)

15 EDEL, Leon, ed. *Henry James: A Collection of Critical Essays*. Englewood Cliffs, N.J., 1963. (By diverse critics.)†

16 EDEL, Leon. "Henry James: The Americano-European Legend." *UTQ*, 36(1967):321–334.

17 EDWARDS, Herbert. "Henry James and Ibsen." *AL*, 24(1952):208–223.

18 ELIOT, T. S. "The Hawthorne Aspect" [of Henry James]. *LitRev*, 5(1958):44–53.

19 ELIOT, T. S. "On Henry James." Repr. in *The Question of Henry James*. Ed. by F. W. Dupee. New York, 1945. (This and another essay by Eliot on James are repr. in *The Shock of Recognition*. Ed. by Edmund Wilson. New York, 1943.)

1 FOLEY, Richard N. *Criticism in American Periodicals of the Works of Henry James from 1866 to 1916.* Washington, D.C., 1944.

2 GALE, Robert L. *The Caught Image: Figurative Language in the Fiction of Henry James.* Chapel Hill, N.C., 1964. (Includes earlier articles on topics such as imagistic patterns relating to art, to religion, etc.)

3 GALE, Robert L. *Plots and Characters in the Fiction of Henry James.* Hamden, Conn., 1965. (Includes short stories.)

4 GEISMAR, Maxwell D. *Henry James and the Jacobites.* Boston, 1963. (Sums up most of what can be said against James.)

5 GOLDSMITH, Arnold. "Henry James's Reconciliation of Free Will and Fatalism." *NCF*, 13(1958):109–126.

6 GOODE, John. "The Art of Fiction: Walter Besant and Henry James." In *Tradition and Tolerance in Nineteenth Century Fiction.* Ed. by David Howard et al. New York, 1966.

7 HARLOW, Virginia. "Thomas Sargeant Perry and Henry James." *BPLQ*, 1(1949):43–60.

8 HOLDER, Alan. "Three Voyagers in Search of Europe: A Study of Henry James, Ezra Pound, and T. S. Eliot." *DA*, 26(1965):1646–1647.

9 HOLLAND, Laurence B. *The Expense of Vision: Essays on the Craft of Henry James.* Princeton, 1964.

10 HOWELLS, W. D. *Discovery of Genius: William Dean Howells and Henry James.* Ed. by Albert Mordell. New York, 1961. (Reprints Howells's essays and reviews relating to James.)

11 HOWELLS, W. D. "Mr. Henry James' Later Work." *NAR*, 173(1903): 125–137, 203, 572–584.

12 KANE, Patricia. "Mutual Perspective: James and Howells as Critics of Each Other's Fiction." *MinnR*, 7(1967):331–341.

13 KELLEY, Cornelia P. *The Early Development of Henry James.* Urbana, Ill., 1930. (Includes tales and criticism.)†

14 KIMBROUGH, Robert, ed. *"The Turn of the Screw."* . . . *Essays in Criticism.* New York, 1966. (Essays by diverse critics.)

15 KROOK, Dorothea. *The Ordeal of Consciousness in Henry James.* Cambridge, Eng., 1962.

16 LEAVIS, F. R. *The Great Tradition: George Eliot, Henry James, Joseph Conrad.* London, 1948; N.Y., 1963.†

17 LEAVIS, F. R. "Henry James and the Function of Criticism." *Scrutiny*, 15(1948):98–104.

18 LeCLAIR, Robert C. *Young Henry James, 1843–1870.* New York, 1955.

19 LeCLAIR, Robert C. *Three American Travellers in England: James Russell Lowell, Henry Adams, and Henry James.* Philadelphia, 1945.

20 LOWREY, Bruce. *Marcel Proust et Henry James: Une Confrontation.* Paris, 1964.

21 MATTHIESSEN, F. O. *American Renaissance.* New York, 1941.†

1 MATTHIESSEN, F. O. *Henry James: The Major Phase.* New York, 1944.†

2 MATTHIESSEN, F. O. *The James Family, Including Selections from the Writings of Henry James, Senior, William, Henry, and Alice James.* New York, 1947.

3 McCARTHY, H. T. *Henry James: The Creative Process.* New York, 1958. (On aesthetic theory.)

4 McELDERRY, Bruce. *Henry James.* New York, 1965.†

5 McLEAN, Robert C. "'The disappointed observer' of *Madame de Mauves.*" *RS*, 33(1965):181–196.

6 MURRAY, Donald. "Henry James and the English Reviewers, 1882–1890." *AL*, 24(1952):1–20.

7 NOWELL-SMITH, Simon. *The Legend of the Master.* London, 1947. (Quotes a multitude of side-lights by diverse acquaintances.)

8 PACEY, W. C. D. "Henry James and His French Contemporaries." *AL*, 13, (1941):240–256.

9 POIRIER, Richard. *The Comic Sense of Henry James: A Study of the Early Novels.* London, 1960.†

10 POIRIER, Richard. *A World Elsewhere: The Place of Style in American Literature.* New York, 1966. (Includes much on James's style.)†

11 PUTT, Samuel G. *Henry James; A Reader's Guide.* Ithaca, N.Y., 1966.

12 PUTT, Samuel G. "A Henry James Jubilee, II." *CM*, 162(1947):284–297.

13 RAHV, Phillip. "The Heiress of All the Ages." *PR*, 10(1943):227–247.

14 REILLY, Robert J. "Henry James and the Morality of Fiction." *AL*, 39(1967):1–30.

15 ROBERTS, Morris. *Henry James's Criticism.* Cambridge, Mass., 1929.

16 ROURKE, Constance. *American Humour: A Study of National Character.* New York, 1931.†

17 SEARS, Sallie. *The Negative Imagination: Form and Perspective in the Novels of Henry James.* Ithaca, N.Y., 1968.

18 SHERMAN, Stuart P. "Aesthetic Idealism of Henry James." *Nation*, 104(1917):393–399. Repr. in Sherman's *On Contemporary Literature.*)

19 SHORT, R. W. "The Sentence Structure of Henry James." *AL*, 17(1946):71–88.

20 SHORT, R. W. "Some Critical Terms for Henry James." *PMLA*, 65(1950):667–680.

21 STAFFORD, W. T. "Henry James the American: Some Views of His Contemporaries." *TCL*, 1(1955):69–76.

22 STAFFORD, W. T. "James Examines Shakespeare. . . ." *PMLA*, 73(1958):123–128.

1 STAFFORD, W. T., ed. *Perspectives on James's "The Portrait of a Lady"*: *A Collection of Critical Essays.* New York, 1967. (The essays by diverse hands, including James's own views before and after the book, embody much beyond the novel itself.)†

2 STEVENSON, Elizabeth. *The Crooked Corridor: A Study of Henry James.* New York, 1949.†

3 STONE, Edward. *The Battle and the Books: Some Aspects of Henry James.* Athens, Ohio, 1964.

4 VAID, Krishna B. *Technique in the Tales of Henry James.* Cambridge, Mass., 1964.

5 VOLPE, Edmond L. "James's Theory of Sex in Fiction." *NCF*, 13(1958): 36–45.

6 WARD, J. A. *The Imagination of Disaster: Evil in the Fiction of Henry James.* Lincoln, Neb., 1961.

7 WARD, J. A. *The Search for Form in the Structure of James's Fiction.* Chapel Hill, N.C., 1967.

8 WARD, J. A. "Social Criticism in James's London Fiction." *ArQ*, 15(1959):36–48.

9 WARREN, Austin. "Myth and Dialectic in the Later Novels." *KR*, 5(1943): 551–568.

10 WARREN, Austin, ed. Henry James Number of the *Kenyon Review.* 5(1943):481–617.

11 WEGELIN, Christof. *The Image of Europe in Henry James.* Dallas, 1958.

12 WELLEK, René. "Henry James's Literary Theory and Criticism." *AL*, 30(1958):293–321.

13 WIESENFARTH, Joseph. *Henry James and the Dramatic Analogy: A Study of the Major Novels of the Middle Period.* New York, 1963.

14 WILLEN, Gerald, ed. *A Casebook on Henry James's "The Turn of the Screw."* New York, 1960.†

15 WILLETT, Maurita. "Henry James's Indebtedness to Balzac." *RLC*, 41(1967):204–227.

16 WILSON, Edmund. *The Triple Thinkers.* Rev. ed. New York, 1948.†

17 WINNER, Viola H. *Henry James and the Visual Arts.* Charlottesville, Va., 1970.

18 WINNER, Viola H. "Pictorialism in Henry James's Theory of the Novel." *Criticism*, 9(1967):1–21.

19 WINTERS, Yvor. "Henry James and the Relation of Morals to Manners." In *In Defense of Reason.* Denver, 1947. Also in *Maule's Curse.* Norfolk, Conn., 1938.†

20 WRIGHT, Walter F. *The Madness of Art: A Study of Henry James.* Lincoln, Neb., 1962.

Sidney Lanier (1842-1881)

Bibliography

1 GRAHAM, Philip, and F. C. THIES. "Bibliography." In *The Centennial Edition of Sidney Lanier*. Ed. by C. R. Anderson. Baltimore, 1945.

Concordance

2 GRAHAM, Philip, and Joseph JONES. *A Concordance to the Poems of Sidney Lanier*. Austin, Tex., 1939.

Text

3 *The Centennial Edition of Sidney Lanier*. Ed. by C. R. Anderson. 10 vols. Baltimore, 1945. (Includes long introductions to individual works by various authorities.)

Biographies

4 MIMS, Edwin. *Sidney Lanier*. Boston, 1905.
5 STARKE, A. H. *Sidney Lanier: A Biographical and Critical Study*. Chapel Hill, N.C., 1933.

Critical Studies

6 ALLEN, Gay Wilson. "Sidney Lanier." In *American Prosody*. New York, 1935.
7 BEAVER, Joseph. "Lanier's Use of Science for Poetic Imagery." *AL*, 24(1953):520–533.
8 FLETCHER, J. G. "Sidney Lanier." *UKCR*, 16(1949):97–102.
9 FOERSTER, Norman. *Nature in American Literature*. New York, 1923.
10 GRAHAM, Philip. "Lanier and Science." *AL*, 4(1932):288–292.
11 GRAHAM, Philip. "Lanier's Reading." *TexSE*, 11(1931):63–89.
12 GRAHAM, Philip. "Sidney Lanier and the Pattern of Contrast." *AQ*, 11(1959):503–508.
13 HARD, Frederick. "Sidney Lanier: Amateur Shakespearean." In *Shakespeare Celebrated: Anniversary Lectures at the Folger Library*. Ed. by Louis Wright. Ithaca, N.Y., 1966.
14 JONES, H. M. "Sidney Lanier." In *American Poetry*. Ed. by P. H. Boynton. New York, 1918.
15 LEARY, Lewis. "The Forlorn Hope of Sidney Lanier." *SAQ*, 46(1947):263–271.

1   MALONE, Kemp. "Sidney Lanier." *JHAM*, 21(1933):244–249.
2   PARKS, Edd W. *Sidney Lanier: The Man, The Poet, The Critic.* Athens, Ga., 1968.
3   RANSOM, J. C. "Hearts and Heads." *AmR*, 2(1934):554–571.
4   TATE, Allen. "A Southern Romantic." *NewR*, 76(1933):67–70.
5   WARFEL, Harry R. "Mystic Vision in 'The Marshes of Glynn'." *MissQ* 19(1965):34–40.
6   WARREN, R. P. "The Blind Poet: Sidney Lanier." *AmR*, 2(1933):27–45.
7   WEBB, Richard, and E. R. COULSON. *Sidney Lanier, Poet and Prosodist.* Athens, Gar., 1941.
8   WILLIAMS, S. T. "Sidney Lanier." In *American Writers on American Literature.* Ed. by John Macy. New York, 1931.
9   WILSON, Edmund. "Sidney Lanier." In *Patriotic Gore: Studies in the Literature of the American Civil War.* New York, 1962.

Henry Wadsworth Longfellow (1807–1882)

Bibliographies

10   BLANCK, Jacob, ed. *Bibliography of American Literature.* Vol. 5. New Haven, 1969.
11   LIVINGSTON, L. S. *A Bibliography of the First Editions . . . of Henry Wadsworth Longfellow.* New York, 1908.

Texts

12   *The Works of Henry Wadsworth Longfellow.* Ed. by Samuel Longfellow. 14 vols. Boston, 1886–1891.
13   *The Complete Poetical Works of Henry Wadsworth Longfellow.* Ed. by H. E. Scudder. Boston, 1893.
14   *Letters of Henry Wadsworth Longfellow.* Ed. by Andrew Hilen. 2 vols. Cambridge, Mass., 1966.

Biographies

15   LONGFELLOW, Samuel. *The Life of Henry Wadsworth Longfellow.* 2 vols. Boston, 1886. *Final Memorials.* Boston, 1887, Vol. 3.
16   THOMPSON, Lawrance. *Young Longfellow, 1807–1843.* New York, 1938.
17   WAGENKNECHT, Edward. *Longfellow: A Full-Length Portrait.* New York, 1955. (Rev. and condensed as *Longfellow: Portrait of an American Humanist.* New York, 1966.)

Critical Studies

1 ALLEN, Gay Wilson. "Henry Wadsworth Longfellow." In *American Prosody*. New York, 1935.

2 ARMS, George. "Longfellow." In *The Fields Were Green*. Stanford, Calif., 1953.

3 ARVIN, Newton. "Early Longfellow." *MR*, 3(1961):145–157.

4 ARVIN, Newton. *Longfellow: His Life and Work*. Boston, 1963.†

5 BEWLEY, Marius. "The Poetry of Longfellow." *HudR*, 16(1963):297–304. (An attack on Longfellow via Arvin's book.)

6 ELLIOTT, G. R. "Gentle Shades of Longfellow." In *The Cycle of Modern Poetry*. Princeton, 1929.

7 HAMMER, Carl, Jr. "Longfellow's Lyrics 'From the German'." *SCL*, 7(1961):155–172.

8 HARDY, Douglas. "Influence of Finnish *Kalevala* in the Composition of Longfellow's *Song of Hiawatha*." *BYUS*, 4(1962):140–144.

9 HART, Loring E. "The Beginnings of Longfellow's Fame." *NEQ*, 36(1963): 63–76.

10 HATFIELD, J. T. *New Light on Longfellow, with Special Reference to His Relations to Germany*. Boston, 1933.

11 HILEN, Andrew. *Longfellow and Scandinavia: A Study of the Poet's Relationship with the Northern Languages and Literature*. New Haven, 1947.

12 HIRSCH, E. L. *Henry Wadsworth Longfellow*. Minneapolis, Minn., 1964.

13 HOWELLS, W. D. "The Art of Longfellow." *NAR*, 184(1907):472–485.

14 HOWELLS, W. D. *Literary Friends and Acquaintances*. New York, 1900.

15 JOHNSON, Carl L. *Professor Longfellow of Harvard*. Eugene, Ore., 1944.

16 JOHNSON, Harvey L. "Longfellow and Portuguese Language and Literature." *CL*, 17(1965):225–233.

17 JONES, H. M. "Longfellow." In *American Writers on American Literature*. Ed. by John Macy. New York, 1931.

18 KORNBLUTH, Martin L. "Longfellow's *Hyperion* and Goethe's *Wilhelm Meisters Lehrjahre*." *ESQ*, 31(1963):55–59.

19 KRUMPELMANN, John T. "Longfellow's Shakespeare-Studies in Heidelberg." *NS*, 13(1964):405–413.

20 LaFRANCE, Marston. "Longfellow's Critical Prefaces." *CLQ*, 6(1964): 398–402.

21 LONG, O. W. "Goethe and Longfellow." In *Literary Pioneers*. Cambridge, Mass., 1935.

22 MATHEWS, J. C. "Echoes of Dante in Longfellow's Poetry." *Italica*, 26(1949):242–259.

23 MELCHIORI, Barbara A. "Longfellow in Italy, with Unpublished Letters of Longfellow and Howells." *SA*, 12(1966):125–135.

1   MORE, Paul Elmer. "The Centenary of Longfellow." In *Shelburne Essays, Fifth Series*. Boston, 1908.

2   MOYNE, Ernest J. *"Hiawatha" and "Kalevala": A Study of the Relationship between Longfellow's "Indian Edda" and the Finnish Epic*. Helsinki, 1963.

3   MOYNE, Ernest J. "Manabozho, Tarenyawagon, and Hiawatha." *SFQ*, 29(1965):195–203.

4   NEMEROV, Howard. "On Longfellow." In *Poetry and Fiction: Essays*. New Brunswick, N.J., 1963.

5   O'NEILL, J. E. "Poet of the Feeling Heart." In *American Classics Reconsidered*. Ed. by H. C. Gardiner. New York, 1958.

6   PEARSON, N. H. "Both Longfellows." *UKCR*, 16(1950):245–253.

7   POE, Edgar A. "Hyperion." In *The Complete Works of Edgar Allan Poe*. Ed. by J. A. Harrison. New York, 1902. Vol. 10, pp. 39–40. See also "Voices of the Night." Vol. 10, pp. 71–80; "Ballads and Other Poems." Vol. 11, pp. 64–85; "Imitation," "Plagiarism," "Mr. Poe's Reply to Outis," "The Longfellow War." Vol. 12, pp. 41–106; "The Spanish Student." Vol. 13, pp. 54–73.

8   PRITCHARD, J. P. "Horatian Influence on Longfellow." *AL*, 4(1932): 22–38.

9   QUINN, A. H., ed. *The Literature of the American People*. New York, 1951.

10 RULAND, Richard. "Longfellow and the Modern Reader." *EJ*, 55(1966): 661–668.

11 SCHRAMM, Wilbur. *"Hiawatha* and its Predecessors." *PQ*, 11(1932): 321–342.

12 SHEPARD, Odell. *Longfellow*. New York, 1934.

13 TRENT, W. P. "Longfellow." In *The Cambridge History of American Literature*. New York, 1918.

14 VON ABELE, Rudolph. "A Note on Longfellow's Poetic." *AL*, 24(1952): 77–83.

15 WARD, Robert Stafford. "The Integrity of Longfellow's Philosophic Perspective," *Carrell*, 1, ii(1960):5–13.

16 WARD, Robert Stafford. "Longfellow's Roots in Yankee Soil." *NEQ*, 41(1968):180–192.

17 WEBER, Alfred. "Der Autor von 'David Whicher' und das Geheimnis der grünen Brille." *JA*, 10(1965):106–125.

18 WHITMAN, Iris L. *Longfellow and Spain*. New York, 1927.

19 WILLIAMS, Cecil B. *Henry Wadsworth Longfellow*. New York, 1964.†

James Russell Lowell (1819–1891)

Bibliographies

20 COOKE, G. W. *A Bibliography of James Russell Lowell*. Boston, 1906.

1 MILLER, F. DeWolfe. "Twenty-Eight Additions to the Canon of Lowell's Criticism." *SB*, 4(1951–1952):205–211.

Texts

2 *Writings.* The Riverside Edition. 12 vols. Boston, 1890–1892.
3 *Writings.* Standard Library Edition. 11 vols. Boston, 1891. (Scudder's *Life* in 2 vols. added in 1902.)
4 *Complete Poetical Works.* Cambridge Edition. Ed. by H. E. Scudder. Boston, 1897, 1917.
5 *Lectures on the English Poets.* Cleveland, 1897.
6 *Impressions of Spain.* Boston, 1899. (Compiled from the *Diplomatic Correspondence*, by J. B. Gilder, with an Introduction by A. A. Adee.)
7 *The Anti-Slavery Papers of James Russell Lowell.* 2 vols. Boston, 1902. (None of these papers are in Lowell's collected works.)
8 *Early Prose Writings.* With a prefatory note by Dr. Hale . . . and an introduction by Walter Littlefield. London, 1902.
9 *Complete Writings.* Elmwood Edition. Ed. by Charles E. Norton. 16 vols. Boston, 1904.
10 "Letters of James Russell Lowell to W. H. Furness." Ed. by H. H. Edes. *PCSM*, 8(1902–1904):134–137.
11 *The Round Table.* Boston, 1913.
12 *The Function of the Poet and Other Essays.* Ed. by Albert Mordell. Boston, 1920.
13 "Some Forgotten Political Essays by Lowell." Ed. by C. M. Fuess. *PMHS*, 62(1929):3–12.
14 *New Letters of James Russell Lowell.* Ed. by M. A. DeW. Howe. New York, 1932.
15 *Uncollected Poems of James Russell Lowell.* Ed. by Thelma Smith. Philadelphia, 1950.
16 *The Scholar-Friends, Letters of Francis James Child and James Russell Lowell.* Ed. by M. A. DeWolfe Howe and G. W. Cottrell, Jr. Cambridge, Mass., 1952.
17 "The Lowell-Howells Friendship: Some Unpublished Letters." Ed. by James L. Woodress. *NEQ*, 26(1953):523–528.
18 "Some Lowell Letters." Ed. by Philip Graham. *TSLL*, 3(1962):557–582.
19 "Twenty-Seven Poems of James Russell Lowell." Ed. by Martin Duberman. *AL*, 35(1963):322–351.
20 *Browning to His American Friends: Letters Between the Brownings, the Storys and James Russell Lowell.* Ed. by Gertrude R. Hudson. London, 1965.

Biographies

21 BEATTY, R. C. *James Russell Lowell.* Nashville, Tenn., 1942.

1 DUBERMAN, Martin. *James Russell Lowell*. Boston, 1966. (Emphasizes Lowell's personality.)†

2 GREENSLET, Ferris. *James Russell Lowell*. Boston, 1905.

3 HOWARD, Leon. *Victorian Knight-Errant*. Berkeley, Calif., 1952. (On Lowell's early life to about 1855.)

4 SCUDDER, H. E. *James Russell Lowell: A Biography*. 2 vols. Boston, 1901.

Critical Studies

5 ALLEN, G. W. "Lowell." In *American Prosody*. New York, 1935.

6 ALTICK, R. D. "Was Lowell an Historical Critic?" *AL*, 14(1942):250–259.

7 ANDERSON, John Q. "Lowell's 'Washers of the Shroud' and the Celtic Legend of the Washer of the Ford." *AL*, 35(1963):361–363.

8 AUSTIN, James C. *Fields of the Atlantic Monthly: Letters to an Editor 1861–1870*. San Marino, Calif., 1953.

9 BAIL, Hamilton Vaughan. "James Russell Lowell's Ode." *PBSA*, 37(1943): 169–202.

10 BAKER, Paul R. *The Fortunate Pilgrims: Americans in Italy 1800–1860*. Cambridge, Mass., 1964.

11 BLAIR, Walter. "A Brahmin Dons Homespun." In *Horse Sense in American Humor*. Chicago, 1942.

12 BLODGETT, Geoffrey T. "The Mind of the Boston Mugwump." *MVHR*, 48(1962):614–634.

13 BROWNELL, W. C. "Lowell." In *American Prose Masters*. New York, 1909.†

14 CAMPBELL, Killis. "Lowell's Uncollected Poems." *PMLA*, 38(1923): 933–937.

15 CAMPBELL, Killis. "Three Notes on Lowell." *MLN*, 38(1923):121–122.

16 CHAPMAN, E. M. "The Biglow Papers Fifty Years After." *YR*, n.s. 6(1916):120–134.

17 CHRISMAN, L. H. "Permanent Values in *The Biglow Papers*." In *John Ruskin, Preacher, and Other Essays*. New York, 1921.

18 CLARK, George P. "James Russell Lowell's Study of the Classics Before Entering Harvard." *JA*, 8(1963):205–209.

19 CLARK, H. H., and Norman FOERSTER, eds. *James Russell Lowell: Representative Selections, with Introduction, Bibliography and Notes*. New York, 1947.

20 CLARK, Harry H. "Lowell—Humanitarian, Nationalist, or Humanist?" *SP*, 27(1930):411–441.

21 *The Critic*, Feb. 23, 1889. (A special number celebrating Lowell's seventieth birthday.)

22 CUNNINGHAM, Esther Lowell. *Three Houses*. Boston, 1955.

23 DeMILLE, G. E. "Lowell." In *Literary Criticism in America*. New York, 1931.

1   EHRLICH, Heyward. "Charles Frederick Briggs and Lowell's *Fable for Critics.*" *MLQ*, 28(1967):329–341.

2   EMERSON, Edward Waldo. *The Early Years of the Saturday Club 1855–1870.* Boston, 1918.

3   FOERSTER, Norman. "Lowell." In *American Criticism.* Boston, 1928.

4   FOERSTER, Norman. "Lowell." In *Nature in American Literature.* New York, 1923.

5   GIBBS, Lincoln. "A Brahmin's Version of Democracy." *AR*, 1(1941):50–62.

6   GRANDGENT, C. H. "From Franklin to Lowell: A Century of New England Pronunciation." *PMLA*, 14(1909):207–239.

7   GREENSLET, Ferris. *The Lowells and Their Seven Worlds.* Boston, 1946.

8   HENRY, H. T. "Music in Lowell's Prose and Verse." *MusQ*, 24(1924):546–572.

9   HOWE, M. A. DeWolfe. *The Atlantic Monthly and Its Makers.* Boston, 1919.

10 HOWELLS, W. D. "Studies of Lowell." In *Literary Friends and Acquaintance.* New York, 1900.

11 HUDSON, Gertrude Reese, ed. *Browning to His American Friends.* London, 1965.

12 JAMES, Henry. "James Russell Lowell." *AtlM*, 69(1892):35–50. "James Russell Lowell 1819–1891." In Charles Dudley Warner (ed.), *Library of the World's Best Literature.* New York, 1896–1897. Repr. in *The American Essays of Henry James.* Ed. with an Introduction by Leon Edel. New York, 1956.

13 JAMES, Henry. "James Russell Lowell." In *Essays in London and Elsewhere.* New York, 1893.

14 JENKINS, W. G. "Lowell's Criteria of Political Values." *NEQ*, 7(1934):115–141.

15 KILLHEFFER, Marie. "A Comparison of the Dialect of the 'Biglow Papers' with the Dialect of Four Yankee Plays." *AS*, 3(1928):222–236.

16 KLIBBE, Lawrence H. *James Russell Lowell's Residence in Spain 1877–1880.* Newark, New Jersey, 1964.

17 *Literary World* 16(1885):217–226. (A "Lowell Number.")

18 LOVETT, R. M. "Lowell." In *American Writers on American Literature.* Ed. by John Macy. New York, 1931.

19 MOULTON, C. W. *Library of Literary Criticism*, Vol. 8. Buffalo, N.Y., 1905.

20 NYE, Russel. "Lowell and American Speech." *PQ*, 17(1939):249–256.

21 PARRINGTON, V. L. "Lowell, Cambridge Brahmin." In *The Romantic Revolution in America.* New York, 1927.

22 PEARCE, Roy Harvey. *The Continuity of American Poetry.* Princeton, 1961.†

1 PERRY, Bliss. "Lowell." In *The Praise of Folly and Other Papers*. Boston, 1923.

2 PETTIGREW, R. C. "Lowell's Criticism of Milton." *AL*, 3(1932):457–464.

3 PLETCHER, David M. *The Awkward Years: American Foreign Relations Under Garfield and Arthur*. Columbia, Mo., 1962.

4 POE, Edgar Allan. "Poems of Lowell." *GraM*, 24(1844):142–143. "A Fable for Critics." *SLM*, 15(1849):189–191. Repr. in Poe's *Complete Works*. Ed. by J. A. Harrison. New York, 1902.

5 POLLAK, Gustav. "Lowell: Patriot and Cosmopolitan." In *International Perspective in Criticism: Goethe, Grillparzer, Sainte-Beuve, Lowell*. New York, 1914.

6 PRITCHARD, J. P. "Aristotle's *Poetics* and Certain American Literary Critics." *CW*, 27(1934):81–85, 89–93, 97–99.

7 PRITCHARD, J. P. "Lowell's Debt to Horace's *Ars Poetica*." *AL*, 3(1931): 259–276.

8 QUINN, Arthur H., ed. *The Literature of the American People*. New York, 1951.

9 REILLY, J. J. *James Russell Lowell as a Critic*. New York, 1915.

10 ROBERTSON, J. M. "Lowell As a Critic." *NAR*, 209(1919):246–262.

11 SHEA, L. M. *Lowell's Religious Outlook*. Washington, 1926.

12 SMALLEY, George W. *Anglo-American Memories*. London, 1911.

13 STAFFORD, John. *The Literary Criticism of "Young America": A Study in the Relationship of Politics and Literature 1837–1850*. Berkeley, Calif., 1952.

14 STEDMAN, E. C. "James Russell Lowell." In *Poets of America*. Boston, 1885.

15 TANDY, Jeannette. "The Biglow Papers." In *Crackerbox Philosophers in American Humor and Satire*. New York, 1925.

16 TANSELLE, G. Thomas. "The Craftsmanship of Lowell: Revisions in *The Cathedral*." *BNYPL*, 70(1966):50–63.

17 THAYER, William Roscoe. "James Russell Lowell As a Teacher." *Scribner's* 68(1920):473–480.

18 THORNDIKE, A. H. "Lowell." In *The Cambridge History of American Literature*, Vol. 2. New York, 1918.

19 VANDERBILT, Kermit. *Charles Eliot Norton, Apostle of Culture in a Democracy*. Cambridge, Mass., 1959.

20 VERNON, Hope Jillson, ed. *The Poems of Maria Lowell with Unpublished Letters and a Biography*. Providence, 1936.

21 WAGGONER, H. H. *American Poets*. Boston, 1968.

22 WARREN, Austin. "Lowell on Thoreau." *SP*, 27(1930):442–461.

23 WENDELL, Barrett. "Mr. Lowell as a Teacher." In *Stelligeri and Other Essays Concerning America*. New York, 1893.

1 WILKINSON, W. C. "Mr. Lowell's Poetry," "Mr. Lowell's 'Cathedral'," and "Mr. Lowell's Prose." In *A Free Lance in the Field of Life and Letters.* New York, 1874.

2 WILLIAMS, Stanley T. *The Spanish Background of American Literature.* 2 vols. New Haven, 1955.

3 WILLSON, Beckles. *America's Ambassadors to England (1785–1929).* New York, 1929.

4 WOODBERRY, G. E. "James Russell Lowell." In *Makers of Literature.* New York, 1900.

5 WURFL, G. "Lowell's Debt to Goethe." *PSCS,* 1(1936):1–89.

Herman Melville (1819–1891)

Bibliographies

6 MINNIGERODE, Meade. *Some Personal Letters of Herman Melville and a Bibliography.* New York, 1922.

7 STERN, Milton R. "A Checklist of Melville Studies." In *The Fine Hammered Steel of Herman Melville.* Urbana, Ill., 1957.

8 VANN, J. D., comp. "A Selected Checklist of Melville Criticism, 1956–1968." *Studies in the Novel,* 1(1969):507–535.

9 WILLIAMS, Stanley T. "Melville." In *Eight American Authors.* Ed. by F. Stovall. New York, 1956. Supplemented by J. C. Mathews in 1963 reprint.

Texts

10 *The Works of Herman Melville.* 16 vols. London, 1922–1924. (The only edition of its scope immediately available. Repr. in New York, 1963.)

11 "Journal of Melville's Voyage in a Clipper Ship" [1860]. Ed. by S. E. Morison. *NEQ,* 2(1929):120–125.

12 *Herman Melville: Representative Selections, with Introduction, Bibliography, and Notes.* Ed. by Willard Thorp. New York, 1938.

13 *Complete Works.* Hendricks House Edition. Chicago, 1948– . (While fourteen volumes were projected, only the following have appeared: *The Confidence Man,* ed. by Elizabeth Foster, 1954; *Moby-Dick,* ed. by L. S. Mansfield and Howard Vincent, 1952; *Piazza Tales,* ed. by E. S. Oliver, 1948; *Pierre; or, The Ambiguities,* ed. by H. A. Murray, 1949; *Clarel: A Poem and Pilgrimage in the Holy Land,* ed. by W. E. Bezanson, 1961.)

14 *The Complete Stories of Herman Melville.* Ed. by Jay Leyda. New York, 1949.

15 *Journal of a Visit to Europe and the Levant, October 11, 1856–May 6, 1857.* Ed. by Howard C. Horsford. Princeton, 1955.

16 *Melville as Lecturer.* Ed. with Introduction by M. M. Sealts, Jr. Cambridge, Mass., 1957.

1   *Letters of Herman Melville.* Ed. by M. R. Davis and W. H. Gilman. New Haven, 1960.

2   *Billy Budd, Sailor.* . . . Ed. by Harrison Hayford and Merton M. Sealts, Jr. Chicago, 1962.†

3   *Stories, Poems, and Letters by* . . . *Melville.* Ed. with Introduction by R. W. B. Lewis. New York, 1962.

4   *The Battle-Pieces of Herman Melville.* Ed. by Hennig Cohen. New York, 1964.

5   *Selected Poems of Herman Melville.* Ed. by Hennig Cohen. New York, 1964.

6   *Melville's "Benito Cereno": A Text for Guided Research.* Ed. by John P. Runden. Boston, 1965.†

7   *Moby-Dick: Authoritative Text, Reviews and Letters by Melville, Analogues and Sources, and Criticism.* Ed. by Harrison Hayford and Hershel Parker. New York, 1967.†

8   *The Writings of Herman Melville.* The Northwestern-Newberry Edition. Ed. by Harrison Hayford, Hershel Parker and G. Thomas Tanselle. Evanston and Chicago, 1968– . (In this edition *Typee, Omoo, Mardi, Redburn,* and *White-Jacket* have been issued.)

Biographies

9   ANDERSON, Charles R. *Melville in the South Seas.* New York, 1939.†

10   ARVIN, Newton. *Herman Melville.* New York, 1950.†

11   BERTHOFF, Warner. *The Example of Melville.* Princeton, 1962.

12   BOWEN, Merlin. *The Long Encounter: Self and Experience in the Writings of Herman Melville.* Chicago, 1960.†

13   BRASWELL, William. *Melville's Religious Thought: An Essay in Interpretation.* New York, 1943; new ed. 1959.

14   CHASE, Richard. *Herman Melville: A Critical Study.* New York, 1949.

15   FREEMAN, John. *Herman Melville.* New York, 1926.

16   GILMAN, W. H. *Melville's Early Life and Redburn.* New York, 1951.

17   HOWARD, Leon. *Herman Melville: A Biography.* Berkeley, Calif., 1951. (Based on Leyda's *Log.*)†

18   HOWARD, Leon. *Herman Melville.* Minneapolis, 1961.†

19   HUMPHREYS, Arthur R. *Herman Melville.* Edinburgh, 1962.

20   JAMES, C. L. R. *Mariners, Renegades and Castaways.* New York, 1953.

21   LEYDA, Jay. *The Melville Log: A Documentary Life of Herman Melville.* 2 vols. New York, 1951. New ed., 1969. Supp, II, 901–958.

22   McHANEY, Thomas L. "The Textual Editions of Hawthorne and Melville." *SL,* II(1969):27–41.

1   MASON, Ronald. *The Spirit above the Dust: A Study of Herman Melville.* London, 1951.

2   METCALF, Eleanor Melville. *Herman Melville: Cycle and Epicycle.* Cambridge, Mass., 1953.

3   MUMFORD, Lewis. *Herman Melville: A Study of his Life and Vision.* New York, 1929.†

4   SEDGWICK, W. E. *Herman Melville: The Tragedy of Mind.* Cambridge, Mass., 1944.

5   THOMPSON, Lawrance. *Melville's Quarrel with God.* Princeton, 1952.†

6   WEAVER, Raymond M. *Herman Melville, Mariner and Mystic.* New York, 1921.

Critical Studies

7   ARVIN, Newton. "Melville's Shorter Poems." *PR*, 16(1949):1034–1046.

8   AUDEN, W. H. *The Enchafed Flood: Or the Romantic Iconography of the Sea.* New York, 1950.†

9   BACH, Bert C. "Melville's Theatrical Mask: The Role of Narrative Perspective in his Short Fiction." *SLIT*, I, 2(1969):43–55.

10 BAIRD, James. *Ishmael: The Art of Melville in the Contexts of International Primitivism.* Baltimore, 1956.

11 BARRETT, Lawrence. "The Differences in Melville's Poetry." *PMLA*, 70(1955):606–623.

12 BERNSTEIN, John. *Pacifism and Rebellion in the Writings of Herman Melville.* The Hague, 1964.†

13 BERNSTEIN, John. "'Benito Cereno' and the Spanish Inquisition." *NCF*, 16(1962):345–350.

14 BEWLEY, Marius. *The Eccentric Design: Form in the Classic American Novel.* New York, 1959.†

15 BEZANSON, W. E. "Melville's Reading of Arnold's Poetry." *PMLA*, 69(1954):365–391.

16 BLACKMUR, R. P. "The Craft of Herman Melville." *VQR*, 14(1938):266–282.

17 BREINIG, Helmbrecht. "The Destruction of Fairyland: Melville's 'Piazza' in the Tradition of the American Imagination." *ELH*, 35(1968):254–283.

18 BRODTKORB, Paul, Jr. *Ishmael's White World: A Phenomenological Reading of Moby-Dick.* New Haven, 1965.

19 BROOKS, Van Wyck. *The Times of Melville and Whitman.* New York, 1947.

20 CANADAY, Nicholas, Jr. *Melville and Authority.* Gainesville, Fla., 1968.

21 CANNON, A. D. "Melville's Use of Sea Ballads and Songs." *WF*, 23(1964):1–16.

22 CARLISLE, E. F. "Captain Amasa Delano: Melville's American Fool." *Criticism*, 7(1965):349–362.

23 CHASE, Richard, ed. *Herman Melville: A Collection of Critical Essays.* Englewood Cliffs, N.J., 1962. (By diverse critics.)†

1   CHATFIELD, E. H. "Levels of Meaning in Melville's 'I and My Chimney'."
    AI, 19(1962):163–169.

2   COLWELL, James L. and Gary SPITZER. "Bartleby and 'The Raven':
    Parallels of the Irrational." *GaR*, 23(1969):37–43.

3   DAVIDSON, F. "'Bartleby': A Few Observations." *ESQ*, 27(1962):25–32.

4   DAVIDSON, F. "Melville, Thoreau, and 'The Apple-Tree Table'." *AL*,
    25(1954):479–488.

5   DAVIS, Merrell R. *Melville's Mardi: A Chartless Voyage*. New Haven,
    1952.

6   D'AZEVEDO, W. "Revolt on The San Dominick." *Phylon*, 17(1956):
    129–140.

7   DILLINGHAM, W. B. "'Neither Believer nor Infidel': Themes of Melville's
    Poetry." *Person*, 46(1965):501–516.

8   DIX, W. S. "Herman Melville and the Problem of Evil." *RIP*, 35(1948):
    81–107.

9   DRYDEN, Edgar A. *Melville's Thematics of Form: The Great Art of Telling
    the Truth*. Baltimore, 1968.

10 EHRLICH, H. "A Note on Melville's 'Men who Dive'." *BNYPL*,
    69(1965):661–664. (Phrase from Melville letter refers to Duyckinck, not
    Emerson.)

11 FEIDELSON, Charles. *Symbolism in American Literature*. Chicago, 1953.†

12 FEISS, E. "Melville as a Reader and Student of Byron." *AL*, 24(1952):
    186–194.

13 FINKELSTEIN, Dorothee M. *Melville's Orienda*. New Haven, 1961.

14 FISHER, M. "Melville's 'Bell Tower': A Double Thrust." *AQ*, 18(1966):
    200–207.

15 FOGLE, Richard H. "Melville and the Civil War." *TSE*, 9(1959):61–89.

16 FOGLE, Richard H. "The Monk and the Bachelor: Melville's *Benito
    Cereno*." *TSE*, 3(1952):155–178.

17 FOGLE, Richard H. "The Themes of Melville's Later Poetry." *TSE*,
    11(1961):65–69.

18 FRANKLIN, H. Bruce. *The Wake of the Gods: Melville's Mythology*
    Stanford, 1963.

19 GALE, Robert L. *Plots and Characters in the Fiction and Narrative Poetry
    of Herman Melville*. Hamden, Conn., 1969.

20 GALLOWAY, David D. "Herman Melville's *Benito Cereno:* an Anatomy."
    TSLL, 9(1967):239–252.

21 GARDNER, J. "*Bartleby:* Art and Social Commitment." *PQ*, 43(1964):
    87–98.

22 GEIST, Stanley. *Herman Melville: Tragic Vision and the Heroic Ideal*.
    Cambridge, Mass., 1939.

23 GIBSON, W. M. "Herman Melville's 'Bartleby the Scrivener' and 'Benito
    Cereno'," in *American Renaissance*. Ed. by M. Abot. Frankfurt, 1963.

1 GROSS, Seymour, ed. *A Benito Cereno Handbook*. Belmont, Calif., 1965.†

2 HAND, H. E. "'And War be Done': *Battle-Pieces* and Other Civil War Poetry of Herman Melville." *JHR*, 11(1963):326–340.

3 HAYFORD, Harrison, and Merrel DAVIS. "Herman Melville as Office-Seeker." *MLQ*, 10(1949):168–173, 377–388.

4 HERBERT, T. Walter, Jr. "Calvinism and Cosmic Evil in *Moby-Dick*." *PMLA*, 84(1969):1613–1619.

5 HETHERINGTON, Hugh W. *Melville's Reviewers, British and American Reviewers, 1846–1891*. Chapel Hill, 1961.

6 HIBLER, David J. "*Drum-Taps* and *Battle-Pieces:* Melville and Whitman on the Civil War." *Personalist*, 50(1969):130–147.

7 HILLWAY, Tyrus. *Herman Melville*. New York, 1963.†

8 HILLWAY, Tyrus. "Melville as Amateur Zoologist." *MLQ*, 12(1951): 159–164.

9 HILLWAY, Tyrus. "Melville as Critic of Science." *MLN*, 65(1950):411–414.

10 HILLWAY, Tyrus. "Melville's Geological Knowledge." *AL*, 21(1949): 232–237.

11 HILLWAY, Tyrus, and Luther S. MANSFIELD, eds. *Moby-Dick Centennial Essays*. Dallas, 1953.

12 HOELTJE, H. H. "Hawthorne, Melville and 'Blackness'." *AL*, 37(1965): 41–51.

13 HOFFMAN, Charles G. "The Shorter Fiction of Herman Melville." *SAQ*, 52(1953):414–430.

14 HOFFMAN, D. G. "Melville in the American Grain." *SFQ*, 14(1950): 185–191.

15 HOFFMAN, D. G. "Melville's 'Story of China Aster'." *AL*, 22(1950): 137–149.

16 HOWARD, Leon. "The Mystery of Melville's Short Stories." In *Americana-Austriaca*. Ed. by Klaus Lanzinger. Wien, Stuttgart, 1966.

17 KAPLAN, S. "Herman Melville and the American National Sin: The Meaning of Benito Cereno." *JNH*, 41(1956):311–338; 42(1957):11–37.

18 KAZIN, Alfred. "On Melville as Scripture." *PR*, 17(1950):67–75.

19 KEELER, Clinton. "Melville's Delano: Our Cheerful Axiologist." *CLAJ*, 10(1966):49–55.

20 KEYSSAR, Alexander. *Melville's Israel Potter: Reflections on the American Dream*. Cambridge, 1970.

21 KNOX, G. A. "Communication and Communion in Melville." *Renascence* 9(1956):26–31.

22 LACY, P. "The Agatha Theme in Melville's Stories." *TexSE*, 35(1956): 96–105.

23 LANG, Hans-Joachim. "Melville und Shakespeare." In *Shakespeare: Seine Welt—Unsere du Welt*. Tubingen, 1965.

1   LAWRENCE, D. H. *Studies in Classic American Literature.* New York, 1923.†

2   LEVIN, Harry. *The Power of Blackness: Hawthorne, Poe, and Melville.* New York, 1958.†

3   LEVY, L. B. "Hawthorne, Melville, and the *Monitor.*" *AL*, 37(1965):33–40.

4   LEWIS, R. W. B. "Melville on Homer." *AL*, 22(1950):166–177.

5   LEWIS, R. W. B., ed. *Herman Melville.* New York, 1962.

6   LINDEMANN, J. "Herman Melville's Civil War." *ModA*, 9(1965):387–398.

7   LINDEMANN, J. "Herman Melville's Reconstruction." *ModA*, 10(1966): 168:172. (Post-Civil War opinions.)

8   LUEDERS, E. G. "The Melville-Hawthorne Relationship in *Pierre* and *The Blithedale Romance.*" *WHR*, 4(1950):323–334.

9   LUTWACK, L. "Melville's Struggle with Style: The Plain, the Ornate, the Reflective." *ForumH*, 3, x(1962):11–17.

10   LYNDE, Richard D. "Melville's Success in 'The Happy Failure: A Story of the River Hudson'." *CLAJ*, 13(1969):119–130.

11   MANSFIELD, L. S. "Some Patterns from Melville's 'Loom of Time'." In *Essays on Determinism in American Literature.* Ed. by S. Krause. Kent, Ohio, 1964.

12   MARCUS, M. "Melville's Bartleby as a Psychological Double." *CE*, 23(1962):365–368.

13   MARX, Leo. "Melville's Parable of the Walls." *SR*, 61(1953):602–627.

14   MATTHIESSEN, F. O. *The American Renaissance.* New York, 1941.†

15   MATTHIESSEN, F. O. "Melville as Poet." In *The Responsibilities of the Critic: Essays and Reviews.* New York, 1952.

16   MAYOUX, Jean J. *Melville.* Paris, 1959. (In English.)

17   MILLER, James E., Jr. *A Reader's Guide to Herman Melville.* New York, 1962.†

18   MILLER, Perry. "Melville and Transcendentalism." *VQR*, 29(1953): 556–575.

19   MILLER, Perry. *The Raven and the Whale.* New York, 1947.†

20   MONTAGUE, G. B. "Melville's *Battle Pieces.*" *TexSE*, 35(1956):106–115.

21   MORPURGO, J. E. "Herman Melville and England." *Month*, 4(1950): 180–186.

22   MOSS, Sidney P. "'Cock-A-Doodle-Doo!' and Some Legends in Melville Scholarship." *AL*, 40(1968):192–210.

23   MURRAY, H. A. "In Nomine Diaboli." *NEQ*, 24(1951):435–452.

24   NEWBERY, I. "'The Encantadas': Melville's *Inferno.*" *AL*, 38(1966):49–68.

25   OATES, J. C. "Melville and the Manichean Illusion." *TSLL*, 4(1962): 117–129.

1 OLIVER, Egbert S. "Melville's Picture of Emerson and Thoreau in *The Confidence Man*." *CE*, 8(1946):61–72.

2 OLSON, Charles. *Call Me Ishmael*. New York, 1947.†

3 PARKER, Hershel. "Melville's Salesman's Story." *SSF*, 1(1964):154–158. (On "The Lightning-Rod Man.")

4 PARKER, Hershel, ed. *The Recognition of Herman Melville*. Ann Arbor, 1967. (Essays by diverse critics.)

5 PATRICK, Walton R. "Melville's 'Bartleby' and the Doctrine of Necessity." *AL*, 41(1969):39–54.

6 PAUL, Sherman. "Melville's 'The Town-Ho's Story'." *AL*, 21(1949): 212–221.

7 PHILLIPS, B. "'The Good Captain': A Reading of 'Benito Cereno'." *TSLL*, 4(1962):188–197.

8 PILKINGTON, W. T. "'Benito Cereno' and the American National Character." *Discourse*, 8(1965):49–63.

9 PILKINGTON, W. T. "*Benito Cereno* and the 'Valor-Ruined Man' of *Moby-Dick*." *TSLL*, 7(1965):201–207.

10 PILKINGTON, W. T. "Melville's *Benito Cereno:* Source and Technique." *SSF*, 2(1965):247–255.

11 POENICKE, Klaus. "A View from 'The Piazza': Herman Melville and the Legacy of the European Sublime." *CLS*, 4(1967):267–281.

12 POMMER, H. F. *Milton and Melville*. Pittsburgh, 1950.

13 PUTZEL, M. "The Source and the Symbols of Melville's 'Benito Cereno'." *AL*, 34(1962): 191–206.

14 REINERT, O. "Bartleby the Inscrutable: Notes on a Melville Motif." In *Americana Norvegica*. Ed. by Sigmund Skard and H. H. Wasser. Philadelphia, 1966.

15 ROHRBERGER, M. "Point of View in 'Benito Cereno': Machinations and Deceptions." *CE*, 27(1966):541–546.

16 ROSENBERRY, E. H. *Melville and the Comic Spirit*. Cambridge, Mass., 1955.

17 ROWLAND, Beryl. "Melville's 'Bachelors and Maids': Interpretation through Symbol and Metaphor." *AL*, 41(1969):389–405.

18 RULAND, Richard. "Melville and the Fortunate Fall: *Typee* and Eden." *NCF*, 63(1968):312–323.

19 RUNDEN, John P., ed. *Melville's 'Benito Cereno': A Text for Guided Research*. Boston, 1965.†

20 SCHIFFMAN, J. "Critical Problems in Melville's 'Benito Cereno'." *MLQ*, 11(1950):317–324.

21 SEALTS, Merton, Jr. "Melville's Chimney Reexamined." *Themes and Directions in American Literature: Essays in Honor of Leon Howard*. Ed. by M. F. Shultz et al., Lafayette, 1969.

22 SEALTS, Merton, Jr. "Melville's 'Geniality'." *Essays in American and English Literature*. Athens, 1968.

1   SEALTS, Merton, Jr. *Melville's Reading: A Check List of Books Owned and Borrowed.* Madison, Wis., 1966. (Rev. and enl. version of a study first published in 1948.)

2   SEELYE, John D. *Melville: The Ironic Diagram,* Evanston, Ill., 1970.

3   SHAW, R. O. "The Civil War Poems of Herman Melville." *LH,* 68(1966): 44–49.

4   SHORT, R. W. "Melville as Symbolist." *UKCR,* 15(1949):38–49.

5   SIMON, Jean. *Herman Melville: Marin, Metaphysicien, et Poete.* Paris, 1939.

6   SIMPSON, Eleanor E. "Melville and the Negro: from *Typee* to 'Benito Cereno'." *AL,* 41(1969):19–38.

7   SLATER, J. "The Domestic Adventurer in Melville's Tales." *AL,* 37(1965): 267–279.

8   SMITH, H. F. "Melville's Master in Chancery and His Recalcitrant Clerk." *AQ,* 17(1965):734–741.

9   SOWDER, W. J. "Melville's 'I and My Chimney'." *MissQ,* 16(1963): 128–145.

10   SPRINGER, N. "Bartleby and the Terror of Limitation." *PMLA,* 80(1965): 410–418.

11   STAFFORD, W. T., ed. *Melville's 'Billy Budd' and the Critics.* San Francisco, Calif., 1961. (An anthology of criticism.)

12   STANONIK, Janez. *Moby-Dick, The Myth and the Symbol: A Study in Folklore and Literature.* Ljubljana, 1962.

13   STEIN, W. B. "Melville and the Creative Eros." *LHB,* 2(1960):13–26.

14   STEIN, W. B. "Melville Roasts Thoreau. . . ." *MLN,* 74(1959):251–259.

15   STEIN, W. B. "Melville's Comedy of Faith." *ELH,* 27(1960):315–333.

16   STEIN, W. B. "Melville's Poetry: Its Symbols of Individuation." *L&P,* 7(1957):21–26.

17   STEIN, W. B. "Melville's Poetry: Two Rising Notes." *ESQ,* 27(1962):10–13.

18   STEIN, W. B. "The Moral Axis of 'Benito Cereno'." *Accent,* 15(1955): 221–233.

19   STERN, Milton R. *The Fine Hammered Steel of Herman Melville.* Urbana, Ill., 1959.

20   STERN, Milton R. "Melville's Tragic Imagination: The Hero without a Home." *Patterns of Commitment in American Literature.* Ed. by Marston LaFrance. Toronto, 1967.

21   STEVENS, H. R. "Melville's Music." *Musicology,* 2(1949):405–421.

22   STONE, G. *Melville.* New York, 1949.

23   STRANDBERG V. H. "God and the Critics of Melville." *TSLL,* 6(1964): 322–333.

1 STRAUCH, C. F., ed. "Melville Supplement." *ESQ*, 28(1962):2–30.
2 SUTTON, W. "Melville's 'Pleasure Poetry' and the Art of Concealment." *PQ*, 30(1951):316–327.
3 TANSELLE, G. Thomas. "The Sales of Melville's Books." *HLB*, 57(1969): 195–215.
4 THOMPSON, W. R. "'The Paradise of Bachelors and the Tartarus of Maids': A Reinterpretation." *AQ*, 9(1957):34–45.
5 VANDERHAAR, Margaret M. "A Re-Examination of 'Benito Cereno'." *AL*, 40(1968):179–191.
6 VERUCCI, V. "'The Bell Tower' of Herman Melville." *SA*, 9(1963):89–120.
7 VINCENT, Howard. *Guide to Herman Melville*. Comumbus, Ohio, 1969.
8 VINCENT, Howard. *The Trying-Out of Moby-Dick*. Boston, 1949.†
9 VINCENT, Howard, ed. *Melville and Hawthorne in the Bershires*. Kent, Ohio, 1968.
10 VINCENT, Howard, ed. *Melville Annual, 1965. A Symposium: "Bartleby the Scrivener."* Kent, Ohio, 1966.
11 WAGENKNECHT, E. "Our Contemporary, Herman Melville." *EJ*, 39(1950):121–128.
12 WARREN, Robert Penn. "Melville the Poet." In *Selected Essays*. New York, 1958. (First published in 1946.)
13 WIDMER, Kingsley. "The Perplexity of Melville: *Benito Cereno*." *SSF*, 5(1968):225–238.
14 WILLIAMS, M. L. "Some Notices and Reviews of Melville's Novels in American Religious Periodicals, 1846–1849." *AL*, 22(1950):121–127.
15 WILLIAMS, S. T. "Follow Your Leader: Melville's *Benito Cereno*." *VQR*, (1947):61–76.
16 WILLIAMS, S. T. "Melville," in *Literary History of the United States*. Ed. by R. E. Spiller et al. New York, 1947.
17 WINTERS, Yvor. *Maule's Curse: Seven Studies in the History of American Obscurantism*. Norfolk, Conn., 1938. (Repr. in Winters's *In Defense of Reason*. New York, 1947.)
18 WRIGHT, N. "Form as Function in Melville." *PMLA*, 57(1952):330–340.
19 WRIGHT, N. *Melville's Use of the Bible*. Durham, N.C., 1949.
20 ZIRKER, P. A. "Evidence of the Slavery Dilemma in *White-Jacket*." *AQ*, 18(1966):477–492.
21 ZOLLA, E. "La struttura e le fonti di *Clarel*." *SA*, 10(1964):101–134.

Frank Norris (1870–1902)

Bibliographies

1 FRENCH, Warren. "Frank Norris. . . ." *ALR*, 1(1967):84–89. (Studies about Norris.)
2 GAER, Joseph. *Frank Norris: Bibliography and Biographical Data.* California Literary Research Project, Monograph No. 3, 1934.
3 LOHF, Kenneth A., and Eugene P. SHEEHY. *Frank Norris: A Bibliography.* Los Gatos, Calif., 1959.
4 WHITE, William. "Frank Norris: Bibliographical Addenda." *BB*, 22(1959):227–228.

Texts

5 *The Complete Works of Frank Norris.* 10 vols. Garden City, N.Y., 1928.
6 *The Letters of Frank Norris.* Ed. by Franklin Walker. San Francisco, 1956.
7 *The Literary Criticism of Frank Norris.* Ed. by Donald Pizer. Austin, Tex., 1964. (Includes criticism, 1895–1903.)
8 "The Remaining Seven of Frank Norris' 'Weekly Letters'." Ed. by Richard Davison. *ALR*, 3(1968):47–65.

Biography

9 WALKER, Franklin D. *Frank Norris: A Biography.* New York, 1932.

Critical Studies

10 ÅHNEBRINK, Lars. *The Influence of Emile Zola on Frank Norris.* Cambridge, Mass., 1947.
11 BIENCOURT, Marius. *Une Influence du Naturalisme Francais en Amerique.* Paris, 1933.
12 FRENCH, Warren. *Frank Norris.* New York, 1962.†
13 MARCHAND, Ernest. *Frank Norris: A Study.* Stanford, Calif., 1942.

Critical Essays

14 BIXLER, P. H. "Frank Norris's Literary Reputation." *AL*, 6(1934):107–121.
15 CASSADY, E. E. "Muckraking in the Gilded Age." *AL*, 13(1941):134–141.
16 COOPERMAN, S. "Frank Norris and the Werewolf of Guilt." *MLQ*, 20(1959):252–258.

1 DAVISON, Richard, ed. *Studies in The Octopus.* Columbus, Ohio, 1969. (Useful collection of criticisms.)

2 DILLINGHAM, W. B. *Frank Norris: Instinct and Art.* Lincoln, Neb., 1969.

3 EDWARDS, H. "Zola and the American Critics." *AL,* 4(1932):114–129.

4 FOLSOM, James K. "Social Darwinism or Social Protest? The '*Philosophy*' of *The Octopus.*" *MFS,* 8(1963):393–400.

5 FRANCIS, H. E., Jr. "A Reconsideration of Frank Norris." *EUQ,* 15(1959):110–118.

6 FROHOCK, W. M. *Frank Norris.* Minneapolis, 1968.

7 GEISMAR, M. "Frank Norris: And the Brute." In *Rebels and Ancestors: The American Novel, 1890–1915.* Boston, 1953.

8 GOLDSMITH, A. L. "The Development of Frank Norris's Philosophy." In *Studies in Honor of John Wilcox.* Ed. by A. D. Wallace and W. O. Ross. Detroit, 1958.

9 GRATTAN, C. H. "Frank Norris." *Bookman,* 69(1929):506–510.

10 HOFFMAN, C. G. "Norris and the Responsibility of the Novelist." *SAQ,* 54(1955):508–515.

11 HOWELLS, W. D. "Frank Norris." *NAR,* 175(1902):769–778.

12 JOHNSON, G. W. "Frank Norris and Romance." *AL,* 33(1961):52–63.

13 JOHNSON, G. W. "The Frontier behind Frank Norris' *McTeague.*" *HLQ,* 26(1962):91–104.

14 KAZIN, A. "Progressivism: The Superman and the Muckrake." In *On Native Grounds.* New York, 1942.

15 KAZIN, A. "Three Pioneer Realists." *SRL,* 20(July 8, 1939):3–4, 14–15.

16 KWIAT, J. J. "Frank Norris: The Novelist as Social Critic and Literary Theorist." *ArQ,* 18(1962):319–328.

17 KWIAT, J. J. "The Newspaper Experience: Crane, Norris, and Dreiser." *NCF,* 8(1953):99–117.

18 LYNN, K. S. "Frank Norris: Mama's Boy." In *The Dream of Success: A Study of the Modern American Imagination.* Boston, 1955.

19 LYNN, K. S. "Introduction" to *The Octopus.* Boston, 1958.

20 MARTIN, W. E., Jr. "Frank Norris's Reading at Harvard College." *AL,* 7(1935):203–204.

21 McKEE, I. "Notable Memorials to Mussel Slough." *PHR,* 17(1948):19–27.

22 MEYER, G. W. "A New Interpretation of *The Octopus.*" *CE,* 4(1943): 351–359.

23 MORGAN, H. W. "Frank Norris: The Romantic as Naturalist." In *American Writers in Rebellion from Twain to Dreiser.* New York, 1945.

24 PARRINGTON, Vernon L. *Main Currents in American Thought,* Vol. 3. New York, 1930.†

1 PEIXOTTO, E. "Romanticist Under the Skin." *SRL*, 9(1933):613–615.
2 PIZER, Donald. "Another Look at *The Octopus*." *NCF*, 10(1955):217–224.
3 PIZER, Donald. "The Concept of Nature in Frank Norris' *The Octopus*." *AQ*, 14(1962):73–80.
4 PIZER, Donald. "Evolutionary Ethical Dualism in Frank Norris' *Vandover and the Brute* and *McTeague*." *PMLA*, 76(1961):552–560.
5 PIZER, Donald. "Frank Norris' Definition of Naturalism." *MFS*, 8(1963):408–410.
6 PIZER, Donald. "The Masculine-Feminine Ethic in Frank Norris' Popular Novels." *TSLL*, 6(1964):84–91.
7 PIZER, Donald. *The Novels of Frank Norris*. Bloomington, Ind., 1966.
8 PIZER, Donald. "Romantic Individualism in Garland, Norris and Crane." *AQ*, 10(1958):463–475.
9 WALKER, Don D. "The Western Naturalism of Frank Norris." *WAL*, 2(1967):14–29.
10 ZIFF, Larzar. *The American 1890s*. New York: 1966. Pp. 250–274.

Edgar Allan Poe (1809–1849)

Bibliographies

11 "Bibliography" to Chapter XIV. *Cambridge History of American Literature*. Vol. 2. New York, 1921.
12 CAMPBELL, Killis. "Recent Books About Poe." *SP*, 24(1927):474–479.
13 HEARTMAN, C. F., and J. R. CANNY. *A Bibliography of First Printings of the Writings of Edgar Allan Poe*. Hattiesburg, Miss., 1940; rev. ed., 1943.
14 HUBBELL, J. B. "Poe." In *Eight American Authors: A Review of Research and Criticism*. Ed. by Floyd Stovall. New York, 1956. Supplemented by J. C. Mathews in 1963 reprint.
15 ROBERTSON, J. W. *Bibliography of the Writings of Edgar A. Poe*. 2 vols. San Francisco, 1934.

Concordance

16 BOOTH, B. A., and C. E. JONES. *A Concordance of the Poetical Works of Edgar Allan Poe*. Baltimore, 1941.

Texts

17 *The Complete Works of Edgar Allan Poe*. The Virginia Edition. Ed. by James A. Harrison. 17 vols. New York, 1902.
18 *The Poems of Edgar Allan Poe*. Ed. by Killis Campbell. Boston, 1917.

1 *Edgar Allan Poe: Representative Selections.* Ed. by Margaret Alterton and Hardin Craig. New York, 1935. Reissued with bibliography brought up to date. New York, 1962.†

2 *The Complete Poems and Stories of Edgar Allan Poe, With Selections from his Critical Writings.* Ed. by Arthur H. Quinn. New York, 1946.

3 *The Letters of Edgar Allan Poe.* Ed. by John Ostrom. 2 vols. Cambridge, Mass., 1948.

4 *The Poems of Edgar Allan Poe.* Ed. with an Introduction, variant readings, and textual notes by Floyd Stovall. Charlottesville, 1965.

5 *Poe's Poems*, Ed. by T. O. Mabbott. Vol. I. Cambridge, Mass., 1970.

Biographies

6 ALLEN, Hervey. *Israfel: The Life and Times of Edgar Allan Poe.* 2 vols. New York, 1926. Rev. in 1 vol. New York, 1934.

7 HARRISON, James A. *Life and Letters of Edgar Allan Poe.* 2 vols. New York, 1903.

8 HUNGERFORD, E. "Poe and Phrenology." *AL*, 2(1930):209–231.

9 KRUTCH, Joseph Wood. *Edgar Allan Poe: A Study in Genius.* New York, 1926.

10 LIND, Sidney E. "Poe and Mesmerism." *PMLA*, 62(1947):1077–1094.

11 QUINN, Arthur H. *Edgar Allan Poe: A Critical Biography.* New York, 1941.

12 REIN, S. M. *Edgar A. Poe: The Inner Pattern.* New York, 1960.

13 WOODBERRY, George E. *The Life of Edgar Allan Poe, Personal and Literary, with his Chief Correspondence with Men of Letters.* 2 vols. Boston, 1909.

Critical Studies

14 ALLEN, Michael. *Poe and the British Magazine Tradition.* New York, 1969.

15 ALTERTON, Margaret. *Origins of Poe's Critical Theory.* Iowa City, 1925.

16 ALTERTON, Margaret, and Hardin CRAIG, eds. "Introduction" to *Poe: Representative Selections.* New York, 1935.†

17 ASSELINEAU, Roger. "Introduction" to *Edgar Poe: Choix de contes.* Paris, 1958.

18 BAILEY, J. O. "What Happens in 'The Fall of the House of Usher?'" *AL*, 35(1964):445–466.

19 BANDY, W. T. "Baudelaire et Edgar Poe: Vue Retrospective." *RLC*, 41(1967):180–194.

20 BASLER, Roy P. "The Interpretation of 'Ligeia'." *CE*, 5(1944):363–372.

21 BAUDELAIRE, Charles. *Baudelaire on Poe*, trans. and ed. by Lois and Francis E. Hyslop. State College, Pa., 1952.

1 BAUDELAIRE, Charles. "Edgar Poe, sa vie et ses oeuvres." In *Histoires Extraordinaire par Edgar Poe*. Paris, 1884.

2 BEEBE, Maurice. "The Universe of Roderick Usher." *Person*, 37(1956): 147–160.

3 BENTON, R. P. "The Works of N. P. Willis as a Catalyst of Poe's Criticism." *AL*, 39(1967):315–324.

4 BLACKMUR, R. P. "Afterword" to *"The Fall of the House of Usher" and Other Tales*. New York, 1960.

5 BLAIR, Walter. "Poe's Conception of Incident and Tone in the Tale." *MP*, 41(1944):228–240.

6 BRADDY, Haldeen. *Glorious Incense: The Fulfillment of Edgar Allan Poe*. Port Washington, N.Y., 1968.

7 BROWNELL, W. C. "Poe," in *American Prose Masters*. New York, 1909.

8 BURANELLI, Vincent. *Edgar Allan Poe*. New York, 1961.†

9 CAMBIARE, C. P. *The Influence of Edgar Allan Poe in France*. New York, 1927.

10 CAMPBELL, Killis. "Contemporary Opinion About Poe." *PMLA*, 36(1921):142–166.

11 CAMPBELL, Killis. "Introduction" to *Poe's Tales*. New York, 1927.

12 CAMPBELL, Killis. *The Mind of Poe and other Studies*. Cambridge, Mass., 1933.

13 CAMPBELL, Killis. "Poe in Relation to His Times." *SP*, 20(1923):239–301.

14 CAMPBELL, Killis. "Poe's Knowledge of the Bible." *SP*, 27(1930):546–551.

15 CAMPBELL, Killis. "Poe's Reading." *TexSE*, 5(1925):166–196. "Addenda and Corrigenda." *TexSE*, 7(1927):175–180.

16 CANBY, Henry S. *Classic Americans*. New York, 1931.

17 CANBY, Henry S. "Poe." In *The Short Story in English*. New York, 1909.

18 CARLSON, Eric W. "Symbol and Sense in Poe's 'Ulalume'." *AL*, 35(1963):22–37.

19 CARLSON, Eric W., ed. *The Recognition of Edgar Allan Poe: Selected Criticism Since 1829*. Ann Arbor, 1966.

20 CASALE, Ottavio M. "Poe on Transcendentalism." *ESQ*, 50(1968):85–97.

21 CHARVAT, William. "Poe: Journalism and the Theory of Poetry." In *Aspects of American Poetry: Essays Presented to H. M. Jones*. Ed. by Richard M. Ludwig. Columbus, Ohio, 1962.

22 CHIARI, Joseph. *Symbolism from Poe to Mallarme: The Growth of a Myth*. Foreword by T. S. Eliot. London, 1956.

23 CONNER, F. W. *Cosmic Optimism*. Gainesville, Fla., 1949. (Includes chapter on Poe and science.)

1   COX, James M. "Edgar Poe: Style as Pose." *VQR*, 44(1968):67–89.

2   DAMERON, J. Lasley. "Poe's Reading of the British Periodicals." *MissQ*, 18(1965):19–25.

3   DAVIDSON, Edward H. *Poe: A Critical Study*. Cambridge, Mass., 1957.

4   DeMILLE, George E. *Literary Criticism in America*. New York, 1931.

5   ELIOT, T. S. "From Poe to Valery." *HudR*, 2(1949):327–342.

6   FAGIN, N. Bryllion. "Edgar Allan Poe." *SAQ*, 1(1952):276–285.

7   FAGIN, N. Bryllion. *The Histrionic Mr. Poe*. Baltimore, 1949.

8   FOERSTER, Norman. *American Criticism: A Study in Literary Theory From Poe to the Present*. Boston, 1928.

9   FRENCH, J. C., ed. *Poe in Foreign Lands and Tongues: A Symposium at the 19th Annual Commemoration of the Edgar Allan Poe Society in Baltimore, Jan. 19, 1941*. Baltimore, 1941.

10 GALE, Robert L. *Plots and Characters in the Writings of Edgar Allan Poe*. Hamden, Conn., 1970.

11 GARGANO, James W. "Poe's 'Ligeia': Dream and Destruction." *CE*, 23(1962):337–342.

12 GARGANO, James W. "The Question of Poe's Narrators." *CE*, 25(1963): 177–181.

13 GARRISON, Joseph M., Jr. "The Function of Terror in the Work of Edgar Allan Poe." *AQ*, 18(1966):136–150.

14 GIACCARI, Ada. "La Fortuna di E. A. Poe in Italia." *SA*, 5(1959):91–118.

15 GRAVA, Arnalds. *L'aspect métaphysique dans l'oeuvre litteraire de Charles Baudelaire et d'Edgar Allan Poe*. Lincoln, Neb., 1956.

16 HALLINE, A. G. "Moral and Religious Concepts in Poe." *BuUS*, 2(1951): 126–131.

17 HOUGH, Robert L., ed. *Literary Criticism of Edgar Allan Poe*. With an Introduction. Lincoln, Neb., 1965.†

18 HUBBELL, J. B. "Poe and the Southern Literary Tradition." *TSLL*, 2(1960):151–171.

19 HUBBELL, J. B. *The South in American Literature*. Durham, N.C., 1954.

20 HUTCHERSON, Dudley R. "Poe's Reputation in England and America, 1850–1909." *AL*, 14(1942):211–233.

21 JACKSON, David K. *Poe and the "Southern Literary Messenger."* Richmond, 1934.

22 JACOBS, Robert D. "Poe among the Virginians." *VMHB*, 67(1959):30–48.

23 JACOBS, Robert D. *Poe: Journalist and Critic*. Baton Rouge, 1970.

1   JACOBS, Robert D. "Poe's Earthly Paradise." *AQ*, 12(1960):404–413.

2   JONES, H. M. "Poe, 'The Raven,' and the Anonymous Young Man." *WHR*, 9(1955):127–138.

3   JONES, P. M. "Poe, Baudelaire and Mallarmé." *MLR*, 39(1944):236–246.

4   KELLY, George. "Poe's Theory of Beauty." *AL*, 27(1956):521–536.

5   KIELY, Robert. "The Comic Masks of E. A. Poe." *UMANESIMO*, I(1967):31–41.

6   LASER, Marvin. "The Growth and Structure of Poe's Concept of Beauty." *ELH*, 15(1948):69–84.

7   LEMMONNIER, Leon. *Edgar Poe et les poetes francais*. Paris, 1932.

8   LEVIN, Harry. *The Power of Blackness*. New York, 1958.†

9   MacDONALD, Dwight. "Masscult and Midcult." *PR*, 27(1960):203–233, 589–631.

10 MARCHAND, Ernest. "Poe As a Social Critic." *AL*, 6(1934):28–43.

11 MARKS, A. H. "Two Rodericks and Two Worms: 'Egotism; Or, The Bosom Serpent'." *PMLA*, 74(1959):607–612.

12 MARKS, E. R. "Poe as Literary Theorist: A Reappraisal." *AL*, 33(1961):296–306.

13 MARTIN, Terence. "The Imagination at Play: Edgar Allan Poe." *KR*, 28(1966):194–209.

14 MATTHIESSEN, F. O. "Poe." In *Literary History of the United States*. Ed. by R. E. Spiller et al. New York, 1948.

15 MENGELING, Marvin and Frances. "From Fancy to Failure: A Study of the Narrators in the Tales of E. A. Poe." *UR*, 33(1967):293–298; (1968):34–37.

16 MILLER, J. E., Jr. "'Ullalume' Resurrected." *PQ*, 34(1965):197–205.

17 MILLER, Perry. *The Raven and the Whale*. New York, 1956.†

18 MOLDENHAUSER, Joseph J. "Murder as a Fine Art: Basic Connections between Poe's Aesthetics, Psychology and Moral Vision." *PMLA*, 83(1968):284–297. (See reply by G. R. Thompson.)

19 MOONEY, Stephen L. "The Comic in Poe's Fiction." *AL*, 33(1962):433–441.

20 MORE, Paul Elmer. "The Origins of Hawthorne and Poe," in *Shelburne Essays*, 1st ser. New York, 1904.

21 MOSS, Sidney P. *Poe's Literary Battles: The Critic in the Context of His Literary Milieu*. Durham, N.C., 1963.

22 O'DONNELL, Charles. "From Earth to Ether: Poe's Flight into Space." *PMLA*, 77(1962):85–91.

23 PARKS, Edd W. *Edgar Allan Poe as Literary Critic*. Athens, Ga., 1964.

1 PATTEE, F. L. "Poe." In *The Development of the American Short Story*. New York, 1923.

2 PETTIGREW, R. C. "Poe's Rime." *AL*, 4(1933):151–159.

3 POCHMANN, H. A. *German Culture in America*. Madison, Wis., 1956.

4 *Poe Newsletter* I(1968). (Among many brief studies is included J. A. Robbins "The State of Poe Studies.")

5 POLLIN, Burton R. "Poe and Godwin." *NCF*, 20(1965):237–253.

6 PRESCOTT, F. C. "Introduction," to *Selections From the Critical Writings of Edgar Allan Poe*. New York, 1909.

7 PRITCHARD, J. P. *Return to the Fountains: Some Classical Sources of American Literature*. Durham, N.C., 1942.

8 QUINN, Patrick. "Four Views of Edgar Poe." *JA*, 5(1960):138–146.

9 QUINN, Patrick. *The French Face of Edgar Allan Poe*. Carbondale, Ill., 1957.

10 RANS, Geoffrey. *Edgar Allan Poe*. Edinburgh, 1965.

11 REGAN, Robert, ed. *Poe: A Collection of Critical Essays*. Englewood Cliffs, N.J., 1967. (By diverse critics.)†

12 RICHARD, Claude. "Poe and 'Young America'." *SB*, 21(1968):25–58.

13 ROBINSON, Arthur. "Poe's 'The Tell-Tale Heart'." *NCF*, 19(1965): 369–378.

14 ROBINSON, Arthur. "Order and Sentience in 'The Fall of the House of Usher'." *PMLA*, 76(1961):68–81.

15 ROPPOLO, J. R. "Meaning and 'The Masque of the Red Death'." *TSE*, 13(1963):59–69.

16 SANFORD, Charles. "Edgar Allan Poe: A Blight upon the Landscape." *AQ*, 20(1968):54–66.

17 SMITH, H. E. "Poe's Extension of his Theory of the Tale." *MP*, 16(1918): 195–203.

18 SPITZER, Leo. "A Reinterpretation of 'The Fall of the House of Usher'." *CL*, 4(1952):351–362.

19 STAUFFER, Donald B. "Style and Meaning in 'Ligeia' and 'William Wilson'." *SSF*, 2(1965):316–330.

20 STEDMAN, E. C. "Introductions." In *The Works of Edgar Allan Poe*. Ed. by E. C. Stedman and G. E. Woodberry. New York, 1927.

21 TATE, Allen. *The Forlorn Demon: Didactic and Critical Essays*. Chicago, 1953.

22 TATE, Allen. "The Poetry of E. A. Poe." *SR*, 76(1968):214–225.

23 TAUPIN, Rene. *L'Influence du Symbolisme francais sur la poesie americaine* [from 1910 to 1920]. Paris, 1929.

24 TAYLOR, W. F. "Israfel in Motley." *SR*, 42(1934):330–340.

1 THOMPSON, G. R. "Unity, Death, and Nothingness—Poe's 'Romantic Skepticism'." *PMLA*, 85(March, 1970):297–300. (Reply to Moldenhauser, above.)

2 VIRTANEN, Reino. "The Irradiations of *Eureka:* Valéry's Reflections on Poe's Cosmology." *TSL*, 7(1962):17–25.

3 WAGENKNECHT, Edward. *Edgar Allan Poe: The Man Behind the Legend.* New York, 1963.

4 WALKER, I. M. "The 'Legimate Sources' of Terror in 'The Fall of the House of Usher'." *MLR*, 61(1966):585–592.

5 WERNER, W. L. "Poe's Theories and Practice in Poetic Technique." *AL*, 2(1930):157–165.

6 WHIPPLE, William. "Poe's Political Satire." *TexSE*, 35(1956):81–95.

7 WILBUR, Richard. "Introduction" to *Poe: Complete Poems.* New York, 1959.†

8 WILT, Napier. "Poe's Attitude Toward his Tales." *MP*, 25(1927):101–105.

9 WINTERS, Yvor. "Edgar Allan Poe: A Crisis in the History of American Obscurantism." *AL*, 8(1937):379–401.

10 YOUNG, Philip. "Earlier Psychologists and Poe." *AL*, 22(1951):442–454.

Edwin Arlington Robinson (*1869–1935*)

Bibliographies

11 BEEBE, L., and R. J. BULKLEY Jr. *A Bibliography of the Writings of Edwin Arlington Robinson.* Cambridge, Mass., 1931.

12 HOGAN, C. B. *A Bibliography of Edwin Arlington Robinson.* New Haven, 1936.

13 HOGAN, C. B. "Edwin Arlington Robinson: New Bibliographical Notes." *PBSA*, 35(1941):115–144.

14 LIPPINCOTT, L. *A Bibliography of the Writings and Criticisms of Edwin Arlington Robinson.* Boston, 1937.

15 WHITE, William. "A Bibliography of E. A. Robinson, 1941–1963." *CLQ*, 7(1965):1–26.

Texts

16 *Collected Poems of Edwin Arlington Robinson.* New York, 1937.

17 *Selected Letters of Edwin Arlington Robinson.* Ed. by R. Torrence. New York, 1940.

18 *Letters of Edwin Arlington Robinson to Howard George Schmitt.* Ed. by C. J. Weber. Waterville, Me., 1943.

19 *Untriangulated Stars: Letters of Edwin Arlington Robinson to Harry de Forest Smith, 1899–1905.* Ed. by Denham Sutcliffe. Cambridge, Mass., 1947.

1 *Tilbury Town: Selected Poems of Edwin Arlington Robinson.* Ed. by L. Thompson. New York, 1953.
2 *Selected Poems of Edwin Arlington Robinson.* Ed. by M. D. Zabel. Introduction by James Dickey. New York, 1965.†
3 *E. A. Robinson's Letters to Edith Brower.* Ed. by Richard Cary. Cambridge, Mass., 1968.

Biographies

4 HAGEDORN, Hermann. *Edwin Arlington Robinson: A Biography.* New York, 1938.
5 NEFF, Emery. *Edwin Arlington Robinson.* New York, 1948.
6 REDMAN, B. R. *Edwin Arlington Robinson.* New York, 1926.

Critical Studies

7 ADAMS, R. P. "The Failure of Edwin Arlington Robinson." *TSE,* 11(1961):97–151.
8 ANDERSON, Wallace L. *E. A. Robinson: A Critical Introduction.* Boston, 1967.†
9 ANDERSON, Wallace L. "E. A. Robinson's 'Scattered Lives'." *AL,* 38(1967):498–507.
10 BARNARD, E. *Edwin Arlington Robinson: A Critical Study.* New York, 1952.
11 BARNARD, E., ed. *Edwin Arlington Robinson: Centenary Essays.* Athens, Ga., 1969.
12 CESTRE, C. *An Introduction to Edwin Arlington Robinson.* New York, 1930.
13 COXE, Louis. *E. A. Robinson.* Minneapolis, 1962.†
14 DONALDSON, Scott. "The Alien Pity: A Study of Character in E. A. Robinson's Poetry." *AL,* 38(1966):219–229.
15 FISHER, John H. "Edward Arlington Robinson and Arthurian Tradition." In *Studies . . . in Honour of Margaret Schlauch.* Ed. by Mieczyslaw Brahmer et al. Warsaw, 1966.
16 FUSSELL, E. S. *Edwin Arlington Robinson: The Literary Background of a Traditional Poet.* Berkeley, Calif., 1954.
17 HEPBURN, J. G. "E. A. Robinson's System of Opposites." *PMLA,* 80(1965):266–274.
18 JOYNER, Nancy. "E. A. Robinson's View of Poetry: A Study of His Theory and His Techniques in the Late Narratives." *DA,* 27(1967):2531A–2532A.
19 KAPLAN, E. *Philosophy in the Poetry of Edwin Arlington Robinson.* New York, 1940.
20 LEVENSON, J. C. "Robinson's Modernity." *VQR,* 44(1968):590–610.
21 LOWELL, A. *Tendencies in Modern American Poetry.* New York, 1917.

84   MAJOR AMERICAN WRITERS

1 MORRIS, L. *The Poetry of Edwin Arlington Robinson: An Essay in Appreciation.* New York, 1923.
2 ROBINSON, W. R. *E. A. Robinson: A Poetry of the Act.* Cleveland, 1967.
3 ST. ARMAND, Barton L. "The Power of Sympathy in the Poetry of Robinson and Frost: The 'Inside' vs. the 'Outside' Narrative." *AQ*, 19(1967):564–574.
4 SMITH, C. P. *Where the Light Falls: A Portrait of Edwin Arlington Robinson.* New York, 1965.
5 STOVALL, Floyd. "E. A. Robinson in Perspective." In *Essays on American Literature.* Ed. by Clarence Gohdes. Durham, N.C., 1967.
6 STOVALL, Floyd. "The Optimism Behind Robinson's Tragedies." *AL*, 10(1938):1–23.
7 UNTERMEYER, Louis. *Edwin Arlington Robinson; A Reappraisal.* Washington, D.C., 1963.
8 WAGGONER, H. H. *The Heel of Elohim: Science and Values of Modern American Poetry.* Norman, Okla., 1950.
9 WEEKS, Lewis E., Jr. "E. A. Robinson's Poetics." *TCL*, 11(1965):131–145.
10 WILLIAMS, Stanley T. "Edwin Arlington Robinson." In *Literary History of the United States.* Ed. by Robert E. Spiller et al. New York, 1948.
11 WINTERS, Yvor. *Edwin Arlington Robinson.* Norfolk, Conn., 1946.
12 ZIETLOW, P. "The Meaning of Tilbury Town: Robinson as a Regional Poet." *NEQ*, 40(1967):188–211.
13 ZIFF, Larzer. *The American 1890's: Life and Times of a Lost Generation.* New York, 1966.†

Henry David Thoreau (1817–1862)

Bibliographies

14 ALLEN, F. H. *A Bibliography of Henry David Thoreau.* Boston, 1908.
15 BURNHAM, P. E., and Carvel Collins. "Contribution to a Bibliography on Thoreau, 1938–1945." *BB*, 19(1946–1947):16–18, 37–39.
16 HARDING, Walter. *A Thoreau Handbook.* New York, 1959.†
17 LEARY, Lewis. "Thoreau." In *Eight American Authors.* Ed. by Floyd Stovall. New York, 1956. Supplemented by J. C. Mathews in 1963 printing.
18 WADE, J. S. "A Contribution to a Bibliography from 1909 to 1936 of Henry David Thoreau." *JNYES*, 47(1939):163–203.
19 WHITE, William. "A Henry David Thoreau Bibliography, 1908–1937." *BB*, 16(1938–1939): 90–92, 111–113, 131–132, 163, 181–182, 199–202.

Texts

1 *The Writings of Henry David Thoreau.* Ed. by H. E. Scudder, F. B. Sanborn, Bradford Torrey, and F. H. Allen. 20 vols. Boston, 1906.

2 *The Correspondence of Henry David Thoreau.* Ed. by Walter Harding and Carl Bode. New York, 1958.

3 *Consciousness in Concord.* Ed. by Perry Miller. Boston, 1959. (The text of Thoreau's lost journal with 124-page introduction.)

4 *Thoreau's Walden. A Writer's Edition with Commentaries.* Ed. by Larzer Ziff. New York, 1961. (The commentaries, pp. 261–332, are designed to stimulate composition classes to imitate examples of Thoreau's handling of such matters as "point of view, assumed nature of the audience, relation of what is assumed to what is stated . . . and definition, description, analogy.")

5 *The Variorum Walden.* Ed. by Walter Harding. New York, 1962.†

6 *Collected Poems of Henry Thoreau.* Ed. by Carl Bode. Enl. ed. Baltimore, 1964.†

7 *The Variorum "Civil Disobedience."* Ed. by Walter Harding. New York, 1967.

Biographies

8 ATKINSON, Justin B. *Henry David Thoreau, the Cosmic Yankee.* New York, 1927.

9 BAZALGETTE, Leon. *Henry Thoreau, Bachelor of Nature.* New York, 1924.

10 CANBY, Henry S. *Thoreau.* Boston, 1939.

11 HARDING, Walter. *The Days of Henry Thoreau, A Biography.* New York, 1965.

Critical Studies

12 ADAMS, Raymond. "Thoreau's Literary Apprenticeship." *SP*, 39(1932): 617–629.

13 ANDERSON, Charles R. Introduction to Thoreau in *American Literary Masters.* New York, 1965.

14 ANDERSON, Charles R. *The Magic Circle of Walden.* New York, 1968.

15 ANDERSON, Charles R. "Wit and Metaphor in Thoreau's Walden." In *USA in Focus: Recent Reinterpretations.* Ed. by Sigmund Skard. Oslo, Norway, 1966.

16 BAYM, Nina. "Thoreau's View of Science." *JHI*, 26(1965):221–234.

17 BODE, Carl. "The Half Hidden Thoreau." *MR*, 4(1963):68–80. (Freudian.)

18 BODE, Carl. "Thoreau: The Double Negative." In *The Young Rebel in American Literature.* London, 1959.

19 BONER, W. H. "Mariners and Terreners: Some Aspects of Nautical Imagery in Thoreau." *AL*, 34(1963):507–519.

1   BOWLING, Lawrence. "Thoreau's Social Criticism as Poetry." *YR*, 55(1965):255–264.

2   BRODERICK, J. C. "Imagery in *Walden*." *TexSE*, 33(1954):80–89.

3   BRODERICK, J. C. "The Movement of Thoreau's Prose." *AL*, 33(1961): 133–142.

4   BRODERICK, J. C. "Thoreau's Proposals for Legislation." *AQ*, 7(1955): 285–289.

5   BRUEL, Andrée. *Emerson et Thoreau*. Paris, 1929.

6   BURANELLI, Vincent. "The Case Against Thoreau." *Ethics*, 67(1957): 257–268.

7   CAMERON, K. W. "Thoreau's Harvard Textbooks." *ESQ*, 23(1961): 19–111. (Mr. Cameron has done numerous other useful studies of Thoreau.)

8   CHRISTIE, Arthur. *The Orient in American Transcendentalism: A Study of Emerson, Thoreau, Alcott*. New York, 1932.

9   CHRISTIE, J. A. *Thoreau as a World Traveler*. New York, 1965.

10 COOKE, R. L. *Passage to Walden*. Boston, 1949.

11 CRAWFORD, B. V. "Introduction." In *Thoreau: Representative Selections, with Introduction, Bibliography, and Notes*. New York, 1934.

12 DEDMOND, F. B. "Thoreau and the Ethical Concept of Government." *Person*, 36(1955):36–46.

13 DRAKE, William. "Spiritual Ideas and Scientific Fact: Thoreau's Search for Reality." *TS Booklet*, 19(1963):54–62.

14 FOERSTER, Norman. "Thoreau." In *Nature in American Literature*. New York, 1923.

15 FUSSELL, Edwin. *Frontier: American Literature and the West*. Princeton, 1965.

16 HARDING, Walter. "Five Ways of Looking at *Walden*." *MR*, 4(1962): 149–162.

17 HARDING, Walter. "The Influence of Civil Disobedience." *TS Booklet*, 19(1963):29–44.

18 HARDING, Walter. *A Thoreau Handbook*. New York, 1959.†

19 HARDING, Walter. *Thoreau: Man of Concord*. New York, 1960.†

20 HARDING, Walter. *Thoreau's Library*. Charlottesville, Va., 1957.

21 HARDING, Walter, ed. *The Thoreau Centennial*. Albany: The State University of New York, 1965. (Includes many essays such as Reginald Cook's "A Parallel of Parablists: Thoreau and Frost.")

22 HARDING, Walter, ed. *Thoreau: A Century of Criticism*. Dallas, 1954. (Essays by diverse critics beginning with Lowell.)

23 HICKS, John H., ed. *Thoreau in Our Season*. Amherst, 1966. (A collection of essays by diverse critics.)

24 HOELTJE, H. H. "Thoreau as Lecturer." *NEQ*, 19(1946):485–494.

25 HOUSTON, W. S. "An Index to the First Ten Years of the Thoreau Society Publications." *TSBooklet*, 8(1953).

1 HOVDE, C. F. "Literary Materials in Thoreau's *A Week*." *PMLA*, 80(1965): 76–83.

2 HOVDE, C. F. "Nature into Art: Thoreau's Use of his Journals in *A Week*." *AL*, 30(1958):165–184.

3 HYMAN, S. E. "Henry Thoreau in Our Time." *AtlM*, 178 (Nov. 1946), 137–146. (Reprinted in Harding's *A Century of Criticism*, above.)

4 HYMAN, S. E. "Thoreau Once More." *MR*, 4(1962):163–170. (Comments on six studies such as those by Sherman Paul, Leo Stoller, Harding, and Mark Van Doren.)

5 JONES, Howard M. "Thoreau and Human Nature." *AtlM*, 210(Sept. 1962):56–61. (Repr. in *History . . . in the Nineteenth Century*, Madison, Wis., 1964.)

6 KERN, Alex C. "American Studies and American Literature: Approaches to . . . Thoreau." *CE*, 27(1966): 480–486.

7 KRUTCH, J. W. *Thoreau*. New York, 1948.†

8 LANE, Lauriat, Jr. "On the Organic Structure of *Walden*." *CE*, 21(1960): 195–202.

9 LANE, Lauriat, Jr., ed. *Approaches to Walden*. San Francisco, 1961.†

10 LEARY, Lewis. "Walden Goes Wandering. *NEQ*, 32(1959):3–30.

11 LORCH, Fred. "Thoreau and the Organic Principle in Poetry." *PMLA*, 53(1938):286–302.

12 LYNN, K. S. "Introduction" to Thoreau. In *Major Writers of America*. Ed. by Perry Miller. New York, 1962.

13 LYON, Melvin. "Walden Pond as a Symbol." *PMLA*, 82(1967):289–300.

14 MATTHIESSEN, F. O. *American Renaissance*. New York, 1941.†

15 McLEAN, A. F. "Thoreau's True Meridian: Natural Fact and Metaphor." *AQ*, 20(1968):567–579. (Emphasizes surveying.)

16 METZGER, C. R. *Thoreau and Whitman: A Study of their Esthetics*. Seattle, 1961.

17 MILLER, Perry. "Afterword." In *Walden . . . and . . . Civil Disobedience*. New York, 1960.

18 MILLER, Perry. "Thoreau in the Context of International Romanticism." *NEQ*, 34(1961):147–159.

19 MOLDENHAUER, J. J. "Images of Circularity in Thoreau's Prose." *TSLL*, 1(1959):245–263.

20 MURRAY, James. *Henry David Thoreau*. New York, 1968.

21 PARRINGTON, V. L. *Main Currents in American Thought*. New York, 1927–1930.†

22 PARSONS, Vesta M. "Thoreau's *The Maine Woods:* An Essay in Appreciation." *HudR*, 1(1967):17–27.

23 PAUL, Sherman. *The Shores of America: Thoreau's Inward Exploration*. Urbana, Ill., 1958.

24 PAUL, Sherman. Introduction to *Walden*. Boston, 1957.

1 PAUL. Sherman, ed. *Thoreau: A Collection of Critical Essays.* Englewood Cliffs, N.J., 1962.†

2 PICKARD, John. "The Religion of 'Higher Laws' in *Walden.*" *ESQ,* 39(1965):68–72.

3 PORTE, Joel. *Emerson and Thoreau.* Middletown, Conn., 1966.

4 PRITCHARD, J. P. *Criticism in America.* Norman, Okla., 1965.

5 PRITCHARD, J. P. "Thoreau." In *Return to the Fountains: Some Classical Influences on American Criticism.* Durham, N.C., 1942.

6 RULAND, Richard, ed. *Twentieth Century Interpretations of Walden.* Englewood Cliffs, N.J., 1968. (Essays by diverse critics.)†

7 SCHWABER, Paul. 'Thoreau's Development in *Walden.*" *Criticism,* 5(1963):64–77.

8 SCUDDER, Townsend. "Henry David Thoreau." In *Literary History of the United States.* Ed. by Robert E. Spiller et al. New York, 1948.

9 SEYBOLD, Ethel. *Thoreau: The Quest and the Classics.* New Haven, 1951.

10 SHANLEY, J. L. *The Making of Walden: With the Text of the First Version.* Chicago, 1957. (Includes analysis of Thoreau's revisions.)

11 STEIN, W. B. "*Walden*: The Wisdom of the Centaur." *ELH,* 25(1958): 194–215.

12 STOLLER, Leo. *After Walden: Thoreau's Changing Views on Economic Man.* Stanford, Calif., 1957.

13 STOLLER, Leo. "A Note on Thoreau's Place in the History of Phenology." *Isis,* 47(1956):172–181.

14 STRAUCH, C. F., ed. "A Symposium on Teaching Thoreau." *ESQ,* 18(1961):2–23.

15 TEMPLEMAN, W. D. "Thoreau, Moralist of the Picturesque." *PMLA,* 47(1932):864–889. (On influence of Gilpin. In a rejoinder to Templeman, J. G. Southworth argued that Wordsworth had a more profound influence— see *PMLA,* 49[1934]:971–974.)

16 TORREY, Bradford. "Thoreau" and "Thoreau's Demands on Nature." In *Friends of the Shelf.* Boston, 1906.

17 VAN DOREN, Mark. *Thoreau: A Critical Study.* Boston, 1916.

18 WARREN, Austin. "Lowell on Thoreau." *SP,* 27(1930):442–461.

19 WILLIAMS, Paul O. "The Concept of Inspiration in Thoreau's Poetry." *PMLA,* 89(1964):466–472.

20 WILSON, Lawrence. "The Transcendentalist View of the West." *WHR,* 14(1960):183–191.

21 WOOD, J. P. "English and American Criticism of Thoreau." *NEQ,* 6(1933):733–746.

Walt Whitman (*1819–1892*)

Bibliographies

1 ALLEN, Evie A. "A Check List of Whitman Publications, 1945–1960." In *Walt Whitman as Man, Poet, and Legend.* Carbondale, Ill., 1961.

2 BOWEN, Dorothy, and Philip DURHAM. "Walt Whitman Materials in the Huntington Library." *HLQ*, 19(1955):81–96.

3 GRANT, Rena. "The Livezey-Whitman Manuscripts." *WWR*, 7(1961):3–14.

4 THORP, Willard. "Whitman." In *Eight American Authors: A Review of Research and Criticism.* New York, 1956. Supplemented by J. C. Mathews in 1963 reprint.

5 WELLS, Carolyn, and Alfred F. GOLDSMITH. *A Concise Bibliography of the Works of Walt Whitman.* Boston, 1922.

6 WHITE, William. "Walt Whitman's Short Stories: Some Comments and a Bibliography." *PBSA*, 52(1958):300–306.

Concordance

7 EBY, Edwin C. *A Concordance of Walt Whitman's "Leaves of Grass and Selected Prose."* Seattle, 1949–1954.

Texts

8 *Walt Whitman's Workshop.* Ed. by C. J. Furness. Cambridge, Mass., 1928. (Miscellaneous manuscripts edited with introductions and notes.)

9 *Leaves of Grass by Walt Whitman.* Ed. by Emory Holloway. New York, 1942.†

10 *Walt Whitman's Manuscripts: Leaves of Grass (1860).* Ed. by Fredson Bowers. Chicago, 1955.

11 "Un Inédit de Walt Whitman: 'Taine's History of English Literature'." Ed. by Roger Asselineau. *EA*, 10(1957):128–138.

12 *Complete Poetry and Selected Prose.* Ed. by James E. Miller, Jr. Boston, 1959.†

13 *An 1855–1856 Notebook Toward the Second Edition of Leaves of Grass.* With an introduction by H. W. Blodgett, a foreword by C. E. Feinberg, and additional notes by William White. Carbondale, Ill., 1959.

14 *Walt Whitman's Leaves of Grass: The First (1855) Edition.* Ed. by Malcolm Cowley. New York, 1959.†

15 *The 1860 Edition of Leaves of Grass.* Ed. by Roy Harvey Pearce. Ithaca, N.Y., 1961.

1 *The Collected Writings of Walt Whitman.* New York, 1961– . General editors, Gay Wilson Allen and Sculley Bradley. So far published: Edwin Haviland Miller, ed., *The Correspondence of Walt Whitman,* vol. I, *1842–1867,* (1961), vol. II, *1868–1875,* (1961), vol. III, *1876–1885,* (1964); Floyd Stovall, ed., *Prose Works 1892,* vol. I, *Specimen Days* (1963), vol. II, *Collect and Other Prose* (1964); Thomas L. Brasher, ed., *Early Poems and the Fiction* (1963); Harold Blodgett and Sculley Bradley, eds., *Leaves of Grass: Comprehensive Reader's Edition* (1964). In preparation: Sculley Bradley and Harold Blodgett, eds., *Leaves of Grass: A Variorum Edition.*

Biographies

2 ALLEN, Gay W. *The Solitary Singer: A Critical Biography of Walt Whitman.* New York, 1955. Rev. ed. 1970.

3 ALLEN, Gay W. *Walt Whitman.* New York, 1961.

4 ALLEN, Gay W., ed. *Walt Whitman Abroad.* Syracuse, N.Y., 1955.

5 ALLEN, Gay W. *Walt Whitman as Man, Poet, and Legend.* Carbondale, Ill., 1961.

6 ASSELINEAU, Roger. *L'Évolution de Walt Whitman après la première Edition des Feuilles d'herbe.* Paris, 1954. Translation by the author: *The Evolution of Walt Whitman: The Creation of a Personality* [first half of *L'Évolution.* . . . Cambridge, Mass., 1960. The *Evolution of Walt Whitman: The Creation of a Book* [second half of *L'Évolution.*] . . . Cambridge, Mass., 1962.

7 BARRUS, Clara. *Whitman and Burroughs, Comrades.* New York, 1931.

8 BAZALGETTE, Leon. *Walt Whitman, the Man and his Work,* trans. by Ellen Fitzgerald. Garden City, N.Y., 1920.

9 BINNS, H. B. *Life of Walt Whitman.* London, 1905.

10 BURROUGHS, John. *Notes on Walt Whitman as Poet and Person.* New York, 1867; enl. 1871. (F. P. Hier, in the *American Mercury* in 1924, shows that Whitman wrote parts of this book, and edited other parts.)

11 CANBY, Henry S. *Walt Whitman, an American.* Boston, 1943.

12 HOLLOWAY, Emory. *Whitman: An Interpretation in Narrative.* New York, 1926.

13 HOLLOWAY, Emory. *Free and Lonesome Heart: The Secret of Walt Whitman.* New York, 1960.

14 PERRY, Bliss. *Walt Whitman, His Life and Work.* Boston, 1906; rev. ed., 1908.

15 TRAUBEL, Horace. *With Walt Whitman in Camden.* 5 vols. New York and Carbondale, Ill., 1906–1964.

Critical Studies

16 ADAMS, Richard P. "Whitman: A Brief Revaluation." *TSE,* 5(1955): 111–149.

1 ADAMS, Richard P. "Whitman's 'Lilacs' and the Tradition of Pastoral Elegy." *PMLA*, 72(1957):479–487.

2 ALEGRIA, Fernando. *Walt Whitman en Hispanoamerica*. Mexico City, 1954.

3 ALLEN, Gay W. "Introduction" to *Leaves of Grass*. New York, 1955.

4 ALLEN, Gay W. *Walt Whitman Handbook*. Chicago, 1946; New York, 1957, 1962.

5 ALLEN, Gay W., and Charles DAVID, eds. *Walt Whitman's Poems: Selections with Critical Aids*. New York, 1955.

6 ANDREWS, Thomas F. "Walt Whitman and Slavery: A Reconsideration of One Aspect of His Concept of the American Common Man." *CLAJ*, 9(1966):225–233.

7 ARVIN, Newton. *Whitman*. New York, 1938.

8 ASSELINEAU, Roger. "Introduction" to Whitman. In *American Literary Masters*. Ed. by Charles Anderson. New York, 1965.

9 BAILEY, John. *Walt Whitman*. New York, 1929.

10 BASLER, R. P. "Introduction" to *Walt Whitman's Memoranda During the War & Death of Abraham Lincoln*. Bloomington, Ind., 1962. Facsimile.

11 BEAVER, Joseph. *Walt Whitman, Poet of Science*. New York, 1951.

12 BLODGETT, Harold W. *Walt Whitman in England*. Ithaca, N.Y., 1934.

13 BLUESTEIN, Gene. "The Advantages of Barbarism: Herder and Whitman's Nationalism." *JHI*, 24(1963):115–126.

14 BOWERS, Fredson. "The Earliest Manuscript of Whitman's 'Passage to India' and Its Notebook." *BNYPL*, 61(1957):319–352.

15 BOWERS, Fredson. "The Manuscripts of Whitman's 'Song of the Redwood-Tree'." *PBSA*, 50(1956):53–85.

16 BOWERS, Fredson. "The Walt Whitman Manuscripts of 'Leaves of Grass (1860)'." In *Textual and Literary Criticism*. Cambridge, Eng., 1959.

17 BRADLEY, Sculley. "The Teaching of Whitman." *CE*, 23(1962):618–622.

18 BRISTOL, James. "Literary Criticism in *Specimen Days*." *WWR*, 12(1966): 16–19.

19 BROOKS, Van Wyck. *The Times of Melville and Whitman*. New York, 1947.

20 BROWN, C. A. "Walt Whitman and the 'New Poetry'." *AL*, 33(1961): 33–45.

21 BURROUGHS, John. *Whitman, A Study*. Boston, 1896.

22 CAMBON, Glauco. "Ancora su Whitman." *Aut Aut*, No. 42(1957):469–485.

23 CAMBON, Glauco. "La Parola come emanazione (Note Marginali sullo stile di Whitman)." *SA*, 5(1959):141–160.

24 CAMBON, Glauco. "Walt Whitman in Italia." *Aut Aut*, No. 39(1957): 244–263.

1   CAMBON, Glauco. "Whitman e il mito di Adamo." *Aut Aut*, No. 40(1957): 315–330.

2   CAMERON, K. W. "Emerson's Recommendation of Whitman in 1863: The Remainder of the Evidence." *ESQ*, 3(1956):14–20.

3   CAMPBELL, Killis. "The Evolution of Whitman as Artist." *AL*, 6(1934): 254–263.

4   CAMPBELL, Killis. "Miscellaneous Notes on Whitman." *TexSE*, 14(1934): 116–122.

5   CANBY, H. S. *Classic Americans*. New York, 1931.

6   CAPEK, Abe. "Introduction" to *Walt Whitman: Poetry and Prose*. East Berlin, 1958.

7   CAPEK, Abe. "Walt Whitman: A Centennial Re-evaluation." *Philologica* (Prague), 7(1955):30–45.

8   CHARI, V. K. "Whitman and Indian Thought." *WHR*, 13(1959):291–302.

9   CHARI, V. K. *Whitman in the Light of Vedantic Mysticism: An Interpretation*. Lincoln, Neb., 1964.

10 CHASE, Richard. "Foreword" to *Specimen Days*. New York, 1961.

11 CHASE, Richard. *Walt Whitman*. Minneapolis, 1961.†

12 CHASE, Richard. *Walt Whitman Reconsidered*. New York, 1955.†

13 CHUPACK, Henry. "Walt Whitman and the Camden Circle." *PNJHS*, 73(1955):274–299.

14 CLARK, Leadie M. *Walt Whitman's Concept of the American Common Man*. New York, 1955.

15 COFFMAN, S. K., Jr. "Form and Meaning in Whitman's 'Passage to India'." *PMLA*, 70(1955):337–349.

16 COOKE, Alice L. "Whitman as a Critic: *Democratic Vistas* with Special Reference to Carlyle." *WWN*, 4(1958):91–95.

17 COOKE, Alice L. "Whitman's Background in the Industrial Movements of His Time." *TexSE*, 15(1935):76–91.

18 COWLEY, Malcolm. "Introduction" to *Leaves of Grass: The First (1855) Edition*. New York, 1959.

19 COWLEY, Malcolm. "Walt Whitman's Buried Masterpiece." *SatR*, 42(Oct. 31, 1959):11–13, 32–34.

20 DAICHES, David. "Imagery and Mood in Tennyson and Whitman." *English Studies Today* (Bern), ser. 2(1961):217–232.

21 DAICHES, David. "Walt Whitman as Innovator." In *The Young Rebel in American Literature*. Ed. by Carl Bode. London, 1959.

22 DAVIS, C. T. "Walt Whitman and the Problem of an American Culture." *CLAJ*, 5(1961):1–16.

23 DE SELINCOURT, Basil. *Walt Whitman: A Critical Study*. London, 1914.

24 DUTTON, Geoffrey. *Walt Whitman*. Edinburgh, 1961.

25 ENGLEKIRK, J. E. "Whitman en castellano." *Atlántico* (Madrid), No. 2(1956):73–87.

1 FALK, R. P. "Walt Whitman and German Thought." *JEGP*, 40(1941): 315–330. (See Parsons.)

2 FANER, R. D. *Walt Whitman and Opera*. Philadelphia, 1951.

3 FAUSETT, Hugh L'Anson. *Walt Whitman: Poet of Democracy*. New Haven, 1942.

4 FIEDLER, L. A. "Introduction" to *Whitman*. New York, 1959.

5 FLEISHER, Frederic. "Walt Whitman's Swedish Reception." *WWN*, 3(1957):19–22, 44–47, 58–62.

6 FOERSTER, Norman. "Whitman." In *American Criticism*. Boston, 1928.

7 FOERSTER, Norman. "Whitman." In *Nature in American Literature*. New York, 1923.

8 FORREY, Robert. "Whitman and the Freudians." *Mainstream*, 14(1961): 45–52.

9 FRANCIS, K. H. "Walt Whitman's French." *MLR*, 51(1956):493–506.

10 FURNESS, C. J. "Walt Whitman's Estimate of Shakespeare." *HSNPL*, 14(1932):1–33.

11 FUSSELL, Edwin. *The Frontier: American Literature and the American West*. Princeton, 1965.

12 GARCÍA BLANCO, Manuel. "Walt Whitman y Unamuno." *Cultura Universitaria* (Venezuela), No. 52(1955):76–102.

13 GARGANO, James W. "Technique in 'Crossing Brooklyn Ferry': The Everlasting Moment." *JEGP*, 62(1963):262–269.

14 GOHDES, Clarence. "Whitman and Emerson." *SR*, 37(1929):79–93.

15 GOLDFARB, Clare R. "The Poet's Role in 'Passage to India'." *WWR*, 8(1962):75–79.

16 GRIFFIN, R. J. "Notes on Structural Devices in Whitman's Poetry." *TSL*, 6(1961):15–24.

17 GRIFFITH, Clark. "Sex and Death: The Significance of Whitman's *Calamus* Themes." *PQ*, 39(1960):18–38.

18 HERRA, Maurice. "Feuilles d'Herbe en Europe et en Amérique Latine." *Europe*, 33(1955):137–145.

19 HINDUS, Milton, ed. *Leaves of Grass One Hundred Years After*. Stanford, Calif., 1955† ,

20 HOLLIS, C. C. "Names in *Leaves of Grass*." *Names*, 5(1957):129–156.

21 HOLLIS, C. C. "Whitman and the American Idiom." *QJS*, 43(1957): 408–420.

22 HOWARTH, Herbert. "Whitman and the Irish Writers." In *Comparative Literature: Proceedings of the Second Congress of the International Comparative Literature Association*. Chapel Hill, N.C., 1960.

23 HOWELL, A. C. "Walt Whitman, Singer of the American Spirit." *ELL*, 4(1957):265–278.

24 IDZERDA, S. J. "Walt Whitman, Politician." *NYH*, 37(1956):171–184.

1 JEFFARES, A. N. "Whitman: The Barbaric Yawp." In *The Great Experiment in American Literature: Six Lectures.* Ed. by Carl Bode. London, 1961.

2 JONES, Joseph. "Carlyle, Whitman, and the Democratic Dilemma." *ESA*, 3(1960):179–197.

3 JOUVENAL, Renaud de. "Walt Whitman." *Europe*, 33(1955):91–107.

4 KAHN, S. J. "The American Backgrounds of Whitman's Sense of Evil." *Scripta Hierosolyminata*, 2(1955):82–118.

5 KAHN, S. J. "Whitman's 'Black Lucifer': Some Possible Sources." *PMLA*, 71(1956):932–944.

6 KRAUSE, S. J. "Whitman, Music, and 'Proud Music of the Storm'." *PMLA*, 72(1957):705–721.

7 LAUTER, Paul. "Walt Whitman: Lover and Comrade." *AI*, 16(1959): 407–435.

8 LAWRENCE, D. H. "Whitman." In *Studies in Classic American Literature.* New York, 1923.

9 LEWIS, R. W. B. "Whitman." In *Major Writers of America.* Ed. by Perry Miller. New York, 1962.

10 LEWIS, R. W. B., ed. *The Presence of Walt Whitman: Selected Papers from the English Institute.* New York, 1962.

11 LIEBERMAN, Elias. "Walt Whitman." In *Great American Liberals.* Ed. by G. R. Mason. Boston, 1956.

12 LOVELL, John, Jr. "Appreciating Whitman: 'Passage to India'." *MLQ*, 21(1960):131–141.

13 LOWENFELS, Walter, and Nan BRAYMER, eds. *Walt Whitman's Civil War.* New York, 1960.

14 MARX, Leo. "The Vernacular Tradition in American Literature: Walt Whitman and Mark Twain." *NS*, 3(1958):46–57.

15 MATSUHARA, Iwao. "Walt Whitman in Japan: From the First Introduction to the Present." *TCEL*, 29(1957):5–42.

16 MATTHIESEN, F. O. "Whitman," in *American Renaissance: Art and Expression in the Age of Emerson and Whitman.* New York, 1941.

17 McLEOD, A. L. "Walt Whitman in Australia." *WWR*, 7(1961):23–35.

18 MILLER, E. H. *Walt Whitman's Poetry: A Psychological Journey.* Boston, 1968.

19 MILLER, E. H., ed. *A Century of Whitman Criticism.* Bloomington, Inda., 1969.

20 MILLER, E. H. and Roselind, Comps. *Walt Whitman's Correspondence: A Checklist.* New York, 1957.

21 MILLER, F. D. "Before The Good Gray Poet." *TSL*, 3(1958):89–98.

22 MILLER, F. D. "Introduction" to *Walt Whitman's Drum-Taps (1865) and Sequel to Drum-Taps (1865–1866).* Gainesville, Fla., 1959.

1 MILLER, J. E., Jr. *A Critical Guide to "Leaves of Grass."* Chicago, 1957.†

2 MILLER, J. E., Jr. "Introduction" to *Walt Whitman: Complete Poetry and Selected Prose.* Boston, 1959.

3 MILLER, J. E., Jr. *Walt Whitman.* New York, 1962.†

4 MILLER, J. E., Jr. "Whitman and Eliot: The Poetry of Mysticism," *SWR,* 43(1958):113–123.

5 MILLER, J. E., Jr. "Whitman and the Province of Poetry," *ArQ,* 14(1958): 5–19.

6 MILLER, J. E., Jr. "Whitman in Italy." *WWR,* 5(1959):28–30.

7 MILLER, J. E., Jr.; Karl Shapiro; and Bernice Slote. *Start with the Sun: Studies in Cosmic Poetry.* Lincoln, Neb., 1960.†

8 MITCHELL, Roger. "A Prosody for Whitman." *PMLA,* 84(1969): 1606–1612.

9 MORE, Paul E. "Walt Whitman." In *Shelburne Essays,* 4th ser. New York, 1906.

10 MORRIS, L. S. "Walt Whitman, o Poeta da Identidade." *Kriterion,* 40/41(1958):438–452.

11 OLIVER, E. S. "The Seas Are All Cross'd': Whitman on America and World Freedom." *WHR,* 9(1955):303–312.

12 OTA, Saburo. "Walt Whitman and Japanese Literature." In *Asia and the Humanities.* Bloomington, Ind., 1959.

13 PARRINGTON, V. L. "The Afterglow of the Enlightenment—Walt Whitman." In *The Beginnings of Critical Realism in America.* New York, 1930.

14 PARSONS, Olive W. "Whitman the Non-Hegelian." *PMLA,* 58(1943): 1073–1093.

15 PEARCE, Roy Harvey. *The Continuity of American Poetry.* Princeton, 1961.†

16 PEARCE, Roy Harvey. "Toward an American Epic." *HudR,* 12(1959): 362–377.

17 PEARCE, Roy Harvey, ed. *Whitman: A Collection of Critical Essays.* Englewood Cliffs, N.J., 1962.†

18 POCHMANN, Henry A. *German Culture in America.* Madison, Wis., 1956.

19 PULOS, C. E. Whitman and Epictetus: The Stoical Element in *Leaves of Grass.*" *JEGP,* 55(1956):75–84.

20 RANCHAN, Som P. (Sharma). *Walt Whitman and the Great Adventure with Self.* Bombay, 1967.

21 RANDEL, William. "Walt Whitman and American Myths." *SAQ,* 59(1960):103–113.

22 REISS, Edmund. "Recent Scholarship on Whitman and Dickinson." In *The Teacher and American Literature.* Ed. by Lewis Leary. Champaign, Ill., 1965.

23 REISS, Edmund. "Whitman's Debt to Animal Magnetism." *PMLA,* 78(1963):80–88.

1 RIESE, TEUT. "Walt Whitman als politischer Dichter." *JA*, 3(1958): 136–150.

2 RINGE, D. A. "Bryant and Whitman: A Study in Artistic Affinities." *BUSE*, 2(1956):85–94.

3 RISING, Clara. "Vistas of a Disillusioned Realist." *WWR*, 7(1961):63–71.

4 RODDIER, Henri. "Pierre Leroux, George Sand, et Walt Whitman ou l'éveil d'un poète." *RLC*, 31(1957):5–33.

5 ROSENBERRY, E. H. "Walt Whitman's All-American Poet." *DN*, 32(1959):1–12.

6 ROUNTREE, T. J. "Whitman's Indirect Expression and Its Application to 'Song of Myself'." *PMLA*, 73(1958):549–555.

7 ROY, G. R. "Walt Whitman, George Sand and Certain French Socialists." *RLC*, 29(1955):550–561.

8 SANTAYANA, George. "The Poetry of Barbarism." In *Interpretations of Poetry and Religion.* New York, 1900.

9 SCHYBERG, Frederik, *Walt Whitman*, trans. by Evie Allison Allen. København, 1933; New York, 1951.

10 SHERMAN, Stuart, P. "Walt Whitman." In *Americans.* New York, 1922.

11 SIXBEY, G. L. "'Chanting the Square Deific'—A Study in Whitman's Religion." *AL*, 9(1937):171–195.

12 SMITH, Fred M. "Whitman's Debt to Carlyle's *Sartor Resartus.*" *MLQ*, 3(1942):51–65.

13 SPENCER, Benjamin T. *The Quest of Nationality.* Syracuse, N.Y., 1957.

14 STAVROU, C. N. *Whitman and Nietzsche: A Comparative Study of their Thought.* Chapel Hill, N.C., 1964.

15 STEBNER, Gerhard. "Whitman—Liliencron—W. H. Auden: Betrachtung und Vergleich motivahnlicher Gedichte." *NS*, 9(1960):105–118.

16 STEDMAN, E. C. *Poets of America.* Boston, 1885.

17 STOVALL, Floyd. "Introduction" and "Bibliography." In *Walt Whitman: Representative Selections.* New York, 1934. (Up-dated, New York, 1961.)

18 STOVALL, Floyd. "Leaves of Grass." *UNCEB*, 35(1956):19–29.

19 STOVALL, Floyd. "Main Drifts in Whitman's Poetry." *AL*, 4(1932):3–21.

20 STOVALL, Floyd. "Walt Whitman: The Man and the Myth." *SAQ*, 54(1955):538–551.

21 STROHL, Beverly L. "An Interpretation of 'Out of the Cradle'." *WWR*, 10(1964):83–87.

22 TAKANO, Fumi. "Walt Whitman's Spiritual Pilgrimage." *SELit*, 34(1957):59–75.

23 TANNER, James T. F. "The Lamarckian Theory of Progress in *Leaves of Grass.*" *WWR*, 9(1963):3–11.

1   TODD, E. W. "Indian Pictures and Two Whitman Poems." *HLQ*, 19(1955): 1–11.
2   WAGGONER, Hyatt H. *American Poets*. Boston, 1968.
3   WARE, Lois. "Poetic Conventions in *Leaves of Grass*." *SP*, 26(1929):47–57.
4   WARFEL, Harry R. "'Out of the Cradle Endlessly Rocking'." *TSL*, 3(1958):83–87.
5   WARFEL, Harry R. "Whitman's Structural Principles in 'Spontaneous Me'." *CE*, 18(1957):190–195.
6   WASKOW, Howard J. *Whitman: Explorations in Form*. Chicago, 1966.
7   WESTBROOK, P. D. *The Greatness of Man: An Essay on Dostoyevsky and Whitman*. New York, 1961.
8   WHICHER, S. E. "Whitman's Awakening to Death: Toward a Biographical Reading of 'Out of the Cradle Endlessly Rocking'." *SIR*, 1(1961):9–28.
9   WHITE, William. "The Walt Whitman Fellowship: An Account of Its Organization and a Checklist of Its Papers." *PBSA*, 51(1957):67–84, 167–169.
10 WILEY, Autrey Nell. "Reiterative Devices in *Leaves of Grass*." *AL*, 1(1929):161–170.
11 WILLARD, C. B. "Ezra Pound's Debt to Walt Whitman." *SP*, 54(1957): 573–581.
12 WILLARD, C. B. *Whitman's American Fame*. Providence, R.I., 1950.
13 WILLSON, Lawrence. "The 'Body Electric' Meets the Genteel Tradition." *NMQ*, 26(1956–1957):369–386.

John Greenleaf Whittier (1807–1892)

Bibliography

14 CURRIER, T. F. *A Bibliography of John Greenleaf Whittier*. Cambridge, Mass., 1937.

Texts

15 *The Writings of John Greenleaf Whittier*, Riverside Edition, 7 vols. Boston, 1888–1889.
16 *The Complete Poetical Works of John Greenleaf Whittier*. Cambridge Edition. Ed. by H. E. Scudder. Boston, 1894.
17 PRAY, Frances M. *A Study of Whittier's Apprenticeship*. Bristol, N.H., 1930. (Includes 109 poems written between 1825–1835).
18 *Whittier on Writers and Writing*. Ed. by Edwin H. Cady and Harry H. Clark. Syracuse, N.Y., 1950.

1   *Legends of New England [1831]*. Ed. by John Pickard. Gainesville, Fla., 1965.

Biographies

2   BENNETT, W. *Whittier: Bard of Freedom*. Chapel Hill, N.C., 1941.
3   CARPENTER, G. R. *Whittier*. Boston, 1903.
4   PERRY, B. *John Greenleaf Whittier*. Boston, 1907.
5   PICKARD, John. "John Greenleaf Whittier and Mary Smith." *AL*, 38(1967):478–497.
6   POLLARD, John A. *John Greenleaf Whittier: Friend of Man*. Boston, 1949.

Critical Studies

7   ALLEN, G. W. "John Greenleaf Whittier." In *American Prosody*. New York, 1935.
8   ANDERSON, John, Jr. "The Library of John Greenleaf Whittier." *ESQ*, 34(1964):1–76.
9   ARMS, G. "Whittier." In *The Fields Were Green*. Stanford, Calif., 1953.
10 CAREY, George G. "Whittier's Roots in a Folk Culture." *EIHC*, 104(1968): 3–18.
11 CHRISTY, A. "Orientalism in New England: Whittier." *AL*, 1(1930): 372–392.
12 CLARK, Harry H. "The Growth of Whittier's Mind—Three Phases." In *Memorabilia of John Greenleaf Whittier*. Ed. by John B. Pickard, Hartford, 1968.
13 ERNEST, J. M., Jr. "Whittier and the 'Feminine Fifties'." *AL*, 28(1956): 184–196.
14 FOERSTER, Norman. *Nature in American Literature*. New York, 1923.
15 HOWE, W. D. "Whittier." In *American Writers on American Literature*. Ed. by John Macy, New York, 1931.
16 JONES, H. M. "Whittier Reconsidered." In *History and the Contemporary*. Madison, Wis., 1964.
17 LEARY, L. *John Greenleaf Whittier*. New York, 1961.†
18 LOWELL, J. R. *The Function of the Poet and Other Essays*. Ed. by Albert Mordell. Boston, 1920.
19 McEUEN, K. A. "Whittier's Rhymes." *AS*, 20(1945):51–57.
20 MILLER, Perry. "John Greenleaf Whittier: The Conscience in Poetry." *HarvR* 2, ii(1964):8–24.
21 MORDELL, A. *J. G. Whittier: Quaker Militant*. Boston, 1933.
22 MORE, P. E. "Whittier as Poet." In *Shelburne Essays, Third Series*. New York, 1906.

1   OLSON, Richard. "Whittier and the Machine Age." In *Memorabilia of John Greenleaf Whittier.* Ed. by John B. Pickard. Hartford, 1968. (Contains many articles by others.)

2   PAYNE, W. M. "Whittier." In *Cambridge History of American Literature.* New York, 1918.

3   PICKARD, John B. "Imagistic and Structural Unity in 'Snow-Bound'." *CE,* 21(1960):338–343.

4   PICKARD, John B. *Whittier.* New York, 1961.†

5   PICKARD, John B., ed. *Whittier Newsletter.* 1968–

6   QUINN, A. H. "Whittier." In *Literature of the American People.* New York, 1951.

7   WAGENKNECHT, E. *John Greenleaf Whittier A Portrait in Paradox.* New York, 1967.

8   WAGGONER, H. H. "What I Had I Gave: Another Look at Whittier." *EIHC,* 95(1959):32–40.

9   WEEKS, Lewis, E. Jr. "Whittier Criticism Over the Years." *EIHC,* 100(1964):159–182.

10 WELLS, H. W. "Cambridge Culture and Folk Poetry." In *The American Way of Poetry.* New York, 1943.

11 WENDELL, B. "Whittier." In *Stelligeri and Other Essays.* New York, 1893.

12 WILLIAMS, C. B. *The Historicity of Whittier's Leaves from Margaret Smith's Journal.* Chicago, 1933.

13 WOODBERRY, G. "Whittier." In *Makers of Literature.* New York, 1900.

Lesser American Writers

Thomas Bailey Aldrich (1836–1907)

Texts (*Other than Novels and Plays*)

14 *The Ballad of Babie Bell and Other Poems,* 1859.

15 *Marjorie Daw and Other People,* 1873.

16 *Ponkapog Papers,* 1903. (Includes criticism.)

17 *A Book of Songs and Sonnets,* 1906.

Biography

18 GREENSLET, Ferris. *The Life of Thomas Bailey Aldrich.* Boston, 1908.

Critical Studies

1 MORE, Paul E. "Aldrich." In *Shelburne Essays, Seventh Series*. New York, 1910.
2 PERRY, Bliss. "Aldrich." In *Park Street Papers*. Boston, 1908.
3 SAMUELS, Charles E. *Thomas Bailey Aldrich*. New York, 1965. (Includes Bibliography.)†

George Bancroft (1800–1891)

Texts

4 *Poems*. Cambridge, Mass., 1823.
5 *Prospectus of a School to be Established at Round Hill, Northampton, Massachusetts*. Cambridge, Mass., 1823. (With Joseph Green Cogswell.)
6 *Some Account of the School for the Liberal Education of Boys*. Northampton, Mass., 1825. (With Joseph Green Cogswell.)
7 *The History of the United States from the Discovery of the Continent*. 10 vols. and 25 various eds. Boston, 1834–1875. A Centenary Edition, thoroughly rev. in 6 vols. Boston, 1876–1879.†
8 *Literary and Historical Miscellanies*. New York, 1855.
9 *On the Exchange of Prisoners during the American War of Independence*. New York, 1862.
10 *Nathanael Greene*. Boston, 1867. (A pamphlet.)
11 *History of the Formation of the Constitution of the United States of America*. 2 vols. New York, 1882.
12 *The History of the United States of America, from the Discovery of the Continent*. 6 vols. New York, 1883–1885. (The author's last revision.)†
13 *The Idea of God as Affected by Modern Knowledge*. Boston, 1885.
14 *The Critical Period of American History, 1783–1789*. Boston, 1888.
15 *The Beginnings of New England*. Boston, 1889.
16 *Martin Van Buren to the End of His Public Career*. New York, 1889.
17 *The War of Independence*. Boston, 1889.
18 *Civil Government in the United States*. Boston, 1890.
19 *The American Revolution*. 2 vols. Boston, 1891.
20 *The History of the Battle of Lake Erie and Miscellaneous Papers*. Ed. with a short biographical sketch by Oliver Dyer. New York, 1891.
21 *The Discovery of America*. 2 vols. Boston, 1892.
22 *Old Virginia and Her Neighbors*. 2 vols. Boston, 1897.

1   *A Century of Science, and other Essays.* Boston, 1899.
2   "The Correspondence of George Bancroft and Martin Van Buren." *PMHS*, 62(1909):381–442.
3   BASSETT, J. S. "The Correspondence of George Bancroft and Jared Sparks." *SCSH* 2, ii(1917):67–143.

Biographies

4   DAVIS, A. M. "George Bancroft." *PAAAS*, 26(1891):303–315.
5   GREENE, S. S. "George Bancroft." *PAAS*, n.s. 7(1890–1891):237–256.
6   HOWE, Mark Anthony De Wolfe. *The Life and Letters of George Bancroft.* 2 vols. New York, 1908.
7   NYE, Russel B. *George Bancroft: Brahmin Rebel.* New York, 1944.†

Critical Studies

8   BASSETT, J. S. *The Middle Group of American Historians.* New York, 1917.
9   BURWICK, Fred L. "The Göttingen Influence on George Bancroft's Idea of Humanity." *JA*, 11(1966):194–212.
10 DAWES, N. H. and F. T. NICHOLS. "Revaluing Bancroft." *NEQ*, 6(1933):278–293.
11 JAMESON, J. Franklin. *The History of Historical Writing in America.* New York, 1891.
12 LEVIN, David. *History as Romantic Art: Bancroft, Prescott, Motley, and Parkman.* Stanford, Calif., 1959.
13 SCHILLER, Andrew. "A Letter from George Bancroft." *NEQ*, 33(1960): 225–232.
14 SLOANE, William M. "George Bancroft—In Society, In Politics, In Letters." *CentM*, 11(1887):473–487.
15 STEWART, Watt. "George Bancroft." In *The Marcus W. Jernegan Essays in American Historiography.* Ed. by William T. Hutchinson. Chicago, 1937.
16 WISH, Harvey. *The American Historian.* New York, 1960.†

Edward Bellamy (1850–1898)

Bibliographies

17 BOWMAN, Sylvia. "Bibliography." In *The Year 2000.* New York, 1958.
18 BOWMAN, Sylvia. "Edward Bellamy. . . ." *ALR*, 1(1967):7–12.

Texts

1 Beyond his widely read novels such as *Looking Backward* (1888)† and *The Duke of Stockbridge* (1900)†—about Shays' Rebellion—*Equality* (1897) is a closely-argued treatise, and *The Blindman's World and Other Stories* (1898) represents the reformer's short stories.

Biographies

2 BOWMAN, Sylvia. *The Year 2000: A Critical Biography of Edward Bellamy.* New York, 1958.

3 MORGAN, Arthur. *Edward Bellamy.* New York, 1944.

Critical Studies

4 BLAU, Joseph. "Bellamy's Religious Motivation for Social Reform: A Review Article." *RRel*, 21(1957):156–166.

5 BOWMAN, Sylvia E., ed. *Edward Bellamy Abroad: An American Prophet's Influence.* New York, 1962. (Essays by many scholars on Bellamy's world-wide influence.)

6 COOPERMAN, Stanley. "Utopian Realism: The Futurist Novels of Bellamy and Howells." *CE*, 24(1963):464–467.

7 FORBES, A. B. "The Literary Quest for Utopia, 1880–1900." *SF*, 6(1927): 179–189.

8 KEGEL, C. H. "Ruskin's St. George in America." *AQ*, 9(1957):412–420.

9 McNAIR, E. W. *Edward Bellamy and the Nationalist Movement, 1889–1894.* Milwaukee, 1957. (Part of thesis, Columbia University.)

10 MADISON, C. A. "Edward Bellamy, Social Dreamer." *NEQ*, 15(1942): 444–466.

11 PARRINGTON, V. L. *Main Currents in American Thought*, vol. III. New York, 1954.†

12 PARRINGTON, V. L., Jr. *American Dreams: A Study of American Utopias.* Providence, R.I., 1947.

13 SANFORD, Charles. "Classics of American Reform Literature." *AQ*, 10(1958):295–311.

14 SCHIFFMAN, Joseph. "Edward Bellamy's Altruistic Man." *AQ*, 6(1954): 195–209.

15 SCHIFFMAN, Joseph. "Edward Bellamy's Religious Thought." *PMLA*, 68(1953):716–732.

16 SCHIFFMAN, Joseph. "Mutual Indebtedness: Unpublished Letters of Edward Bellamy to William Dean Howells." *HLB*, 12(1958):363–374.

1   TAYLOR, W. F. "Edward Bellamy." In *The Economic Novel in America.*
    Chapel Hill, N.C., 1942.

Ambrose Bierce (1842–1914?)

Bibliographies

2   FATOUT, Paul. "Ambrose Bierce. . . ." *ALR*, 1(1967):13–19. (Studies
    about Bierce.)
3   STARRETT, Vincent, ed. *Ambrose Bierce: A Bibliography.* Philadelphia,
    1929.

Texts

4   *The Collected Works of Ambrose Bierce*, 12 vols. New York, 1909–1912.
5   *The Collected Writings of Ambrose Bierce.* Ed. by Clifton Fadiman. New
    York, 1946.†
6   *Letters of Ambrose Bierce.* Ed. by Bertha Pope. San Francisco, 1922.
7   *Twenty-one Letters of Ambrose Bierce.* Ed. by Samuel Loveman. Cleveland,
    1922.

Biographies and Critical Studies

8   BAHR, Howard W. "Ambrose Bierce and Realism." *SoQ*, 1(1963):309–331.
9   BOYNTON, Percy H. "Ambrose Bierce." In *Some Contemporary Americans.*
    Chicago, 1927.
10 COOPER, Frederick Taber. *Some American Story Tellers.* New York, 1911.
11 DE CASTRO, Adolphe. *Portrait of Ambrose Bierce.* New York, 1929.
12 FATOUT, Paul. *Ambrose Bierce and the Black Hills.* Norman, Okla., 1956.
13 FATOUT, Paul. *Ambrose Bierce, The Devil's Lexicographer.* Norman,
    Okla., 1951.
14 GOLDSTEIN, Jessie Sidney. "Edwin Markham, Ambrose Bierce, and *The
    Man With the Hoe*." *MLN*, 58(1943):165–175.
15 GRATTAN, Clinton Hartley. *Bitter Bierce.* New York, 1929.
16 GRENANDER, M. E. "Ambrose Bierce, John Camden Hotten, *The Fiend's
    Delight* and *Nuggets and Dust*." *HLQ*, 28(1965):353–371.
17 GRENANDER, M. E. "Bierce's Turn of the Screw: Tales of Ironical
    Terror." *WHR*, 11(1957):257–264.
18 GRENANDER, M. E. "Seven Ambrose Bierce Letters." *YULG*, 32(1957):
    12–18.
19 HALL, Carroll D. *Bierce and the Poe Hoax.* San Francisco, 1934.

1 HARDING, Ruth Guthrie. "Mr. Boythorn Bierce." *Bookman*, 61(1925): 636–643.

2 JORDAN-SMITH, Paul. "Ambrose Bierce." In *On Strange Altars*. New York, 1924.

3 KLEIN, Marcus. "San Francisco and Her Hateful Ambrose Bierce." *HudR*, 7(1954):392–407.

4 McWILLIAMS, Carey. *Ambrose Bierce*. New York, 1929; Hamden, Conn., 1967. (With new Introduction.)

5 MILLER, Arthur E. "The Influence of Edgar Allan Poe on Ambrose Bierce." *AL*, 4(1932):130–150.

6 MONAGHAN, Frank. "Ambrose Bierce and the Authorship of *The Monk and the Hangman's Daughter*." *AL*, 2(1931):337–349.

7 NATIONS, Leroy J. "Ambrose Bierce: The Gray Wolf of American Letters." *SAQ*, 25(1926):253–258.

8 NEALE, Walter J. *Life of Ambrose Bierce*. New York, 1929.

9 NOEL, Joseph. *Footloose in Arcadia*. New York, 1940.

10 O'CONNOR, Richard. *Ambrose Bierce: A Biography*. New York, 1967.

11 PARTRIDGE, Eric. "Ambrose Bierce." *Lond M*, 16(1927):625–638.

12 POLLARD, Percival. *Their Day in Court*. New York, 1909.

13 SMITH, Edward H. "The Ambrose Bierce Irony." In *Mysteries of the Missing*. New York, 1927.

14 SNELL, George. "Poe Redivivus." *ArQ*, 1(1945):49–57.

15 STARRETT, Vincent. *Ambrose Bierce*. Chicago, 1920.

16 STERLING, George. "A Memoir of Ambrose Bierce." In *The Letters of Ambrose Bierce*. Ed. by Bertha C. Pope. San Francisco, 1922.

17 STERLING, George. "Introduction." In *In the Midst of Life*. New York, 1927.†

18 WALKER, Franklin. *Ambrose Bierce, the Wickedest Man in San Francisco*. San Francisco, 1941.

19 WALKER, Franklin. "The Town Crier." In *San Francisco's Literary Frontier*. New York, 1939.

20 WILT, Napier. "Ambrose Bierce and the Civil War." *AL*, 1(1929):260–285.

21 WOODRUFF, Stuart C. *The Short Stories of Ambrose Bierce, A Study in Polarity*. Pittsburgh, 1964.†

John Burroughs (1837–1921)

Texts

22 *Notes on Walt Whitman as Poet and Person*. Cambridge, Mass., 1867. (See the more mature and critical *Whitman: A Study*, 1896, reissued as vol. X in the complete *Writings*.)

23 *The Writings of John Burroughs*. 23 vols. Boston, 1904–1922.

1 *John Burroughs and Ludella Peck.* New York, 1925. (Correspondence, 1892–1912.)
2 *The Heart of John Burroughs' Journals.* Ed. by Clara Barrus. Boston, 1928.

Biography

3 BARRUS, Clara. *The Life and Letters of John Burroughs.* 2 vols. Boston, 1925.

Critical Studies

4 BARRUS, Clara. *Whitman and Burroughs, Comrades.* Boston, 1931.
5 FOERSTER, Norman. "Burroughs." In *Nature in American Literature.* New York, 1923.
6 GARLAND, Hamlin. "My Friend John Burroughs." *Century,* 102(1921): 731–742.
7 HICKS, Philip M. *The Development of the Natural History Essay in American History.* Philadelphia, 1924.
8 LONG, W. J. "The Modern School of Nature Study and Its Critics." *NAR,* 176(1903):688–698.
9 OSBORN, Clifford H. *The Religion of John Burroughs.* Boston, 1930.
10 OSBORN, Henry F. *Impressions of the Great Naturalists.* New York, 1924.
11 PERRY, Bliss. "John Burroughs." In *The Praise of Folly and Other Papers.* Boston, 1923.
12 SHARP, Dallas. "Fifty Years of John Burroughs." *AtlM,* 106(1910):631–641.
13 TRACY, Henry C. *American Naturalists.* New York, 1930.
14 WEST, H. L. "John Burroughs." *Bookman,* 49(1919):389–398.

George Washington Cable (1844–1925)

Bibliography

15 BUTCHER, Philip. "George Washington Cable. . . ." *ALR,* 1(1967):20–25.

Texts

16 *The Negro Question: A Selection of Writings on Civil Rights in the South.* By George W. Cable. Ed. by Arlin Turner. Garden City, N.Y., 1958.†
17 *The Works of George W. Cable.* Ed. by Arlin Turner. New York, 1970. (The first volume of a projected 19 vol. ed. with notes and introduction.)

Biographies

1 BIKLE, L. L. Cable. *George W. Cable: His Life and Letters*. New York, 1928.
2 BUTCHER, P. *George W. Cable: The Northampton Years*. New York, 1959.†
3 EKSTROM, Kjell. *George Washington Cable: A Study of His Early Life and Work*. Cambridge, Mass., 1950.
4 TURNER, Arlin. *George W. Cable: A Biography*. Durham, N.C., 1956.†

Critical Studies

5 ARVIN, N. "Introduction." In Cable's *The Grandissimes*. New York, 1957.†
6 BROOKS, Van Wyck. *The Times of Melville and Whitman*. New York, 1947.
7 CARDWELL, G. A. *Twins of Genius*. East Lansing, Mich., 1953.
8 CHASE, R. "Cable and His Grandissimes." *KR*, 18(1956):373–383. Repr. in Chase's *The American Novel and Its Tradition*. Garden City, New York, 1957.†
9 HUBBELL, J. B. *The South in American Literature: 1607–1900*. Durham, N.C., 1954.
10 PATTEE, Fred L. *Development of the American Short Story*. New York, 1923.
11 RUBIN, L. D., Jr. *George W. Cable: The Life and Times of a Southern Heretic*. New York, 1969.
12 RUBIN, L. D., Jr. "The Road to Yoknapatawpha: George W. Cable and *John March, Southerner*." In *The Faraway Country: Writers of the Modern South*. Seattle, Wash., 1963. (Original version of this essay appeared in *VQR*, 35(1959):119–132.)†
13 STONE, E. "Usher, Poquelin, and Miss Emily: The Progress of Southern Gothic." *GaR*, 14(1960):433–443.
14 TINKER, E. L. "Cable and the Creoles." *AL*, 5(1934):313–326.
15 TURNER, Arlin. *Mark Twain and George W. Cable: The Record of a Literary Friendship*. East Lansing, Mich., 1960.
16 WILSON, Edmund. *Patriotic Gore*. New York, 1962.†

John William De Forest (1826–1906)

Bibliographies

17 HAGEMANN, E. R. "A Checklist of the Writings of John William De Forest (1826–1906)." *SB*, 8(1956):185–194.
18 LIGHT, James F. "John William De Forest. . . ." *ALR*, 1(1967):32–35. (Studies about De Forest.)

Critical Studies

1 CROUSHORE, James H., and David M. POTTER. "Introduction." In *A Union Officer in the Reconstruction*. New Haven, 1948.

2 FALK, Robert. "John W. De Forest: The Panoramic Novel of Realism." In *The Victorian Mode in American Fiction: 1865–1885*. East Lansing, Mich., 1965.

3 HAIGHT, Gordon S. "Introduction." In *Miss Ravenel's Conversion from Secession to Loyalty*. New York, 1939.†

4 LEVY, Leo B. "Naturalism in the Making: De Forest's *Honest John Vane*." *NEQ*, 37(1964):89–98.

5 LIGHT, James F. *John William De Forest*. New York, 1965.†

6 McINTYRE, Clara F. "J. W. De Forest, Pioneer Realist." *UWP*, 9(1942): 1–13.

7 MARIANI, Umberto. "Il realismo di John W. De Forest." *SA*, 7(1961): 77–103.

8 O'DONNELL, Thomas F. "De Forest, Van Petten, and Stephen Crane." *AL*, 22(1956):578–580.

9 RUBIN, Joseph Jay. "Introduction." In *Honest John Vane*. State College, Pa., 1966. (Includes attack on political discussion in Washington.)

10 RUBIN, Joseph Jay. "Introduction." In *Kate Beaumont*. State College, Pa., 1963.

11 RUBIN, Joseph Jay. "Introduction." In *Playing the Mischief*. State College, Pa., 1961. (Washington background.)

12 SIMPSON, Claude M., Jr. "John W. De Forest, *Miss Ravenel's Conversion*." In *The American Novel from James Fenimore Cooper to William Faulkner*. Ed. by Wallace Stegner. New York, 1965.

13 WILLIAMS, Stanley T. "Introduction." In *A Volunteer's Adventures*. New Haven, 1946.

14 WILSON, Edmund. *Patriotic Gore*. New York, 1962.†

John Fiske (1842–1901)

Texts

15 *The Historical Writings of John Fiske*. Standard Library Edition. 12 vols. Boston, 1902.

16 *The Miscellaneous Writings of John Fiske*. Standard Library Edition. 12 vols. Boston, 1902.

Biographies

17 CLARK, John Spencer. *The Life and Letters of John Fiske*. 2 vols. Boston, 1917.

18 PERRY, T. S. *John Fiske*. Boston, 1906.

Critical Studies

1 ANDREWS, Charles M. "John Fiske." *YR*, n.s. 8(1918):865–869.
2 BERMAN, Milton. *John Fiske: The Evolution of a Popularizer.* Cambridge, Mass., 1961.
3 COMMAGER, Henry S. "John Fiske: An Interpretation." *PMHS*, 66(1942):332–345.
4 HART, A. B. "The Historical Services of John Fiske." *IM*, 4(1901):558–569.
5 NYE, Russel B. "John Fiske and his Cosmic Philosophy." *PMASAL*, 28(1943):685–698.
6 PANNILL, H. Burnell. *The Religious Faith of John Fiske.* Durham, N.C., 1957.
7 POWELL, Lawrence C. "John Fiske, Bookman." *PBSA*, 35(1941):221–254.
8 ROYCE, Josiah. "Introduction." In Fiske's *Outlines of Cosmic Philosophy.* Boston, 1902.
9 SANDERS, Jennings B. "John Fiske." In *The Marcus Jernegan Essays in American Historiography.* Ed. by William T. Hutchinson. Chicago, 1937.
10 SAVETH, Edward N. *American Historians and European Immigrants, 1875–1925.* New York, 1948.
11 WISH, Harvey. *American Historian.* New York, 1960.†

Henry George (*1839–1897*)

Text

12 *The Complete Works of Henry George.* 10 vols. New York, 1904.

Biography

13 BARKER, C. A. *Henry George.* New York, 1955. (Pp. 637–682, Bibliography.)

Critical Studies

14 DORFMAN, J. *The Economic Mind in American Civilization.* 5 vols. New York, 1946–1959. (Vol. 4, covering 1865–1918, discusses Henry George.)
15 GEIGER, G. P. *The Philosophy of Henry George.* New York, 1933.
16 JOHNSON, E. N. "The Economics of Henry George's *Progress and Poetry.*" *JPE*, 18(1910):714–735.
17 JOHNSON, G. W. *The Lunatic Fringe.* Philadelphia, 1957. (Among a dozen reformers this includes T. R. Roosevelt and Henry George.)

1   LAWRENCE, E. P. *Henry George in the British Isles.* East Lansing, Mich., 1957.
2   MADISON, C. A. *Critics and Crusaders: A Century of American Protest.* New York, 1947. (Sketches of 15 dissenters.)
3   PARRINGTON, V. L. *Main Currents in American Thought.* Vol. 3. New York, 1954.†
4   SAKOLSKI, A. M. *Land Tenure and Land Taxation in America, 1607–1879.* New York, 1957.
5   TOYNBEE, Arnold. *"Progress and Poverty": A Criticism of Mr. Henry George.* London, 1883.
6   YOUNG, A. N. *The Single Tax Movement in the U.S.* Princeton, 1916.

Bret Harte *(1836–1902)*

Bibliography

7   STEWART, G. R. *A Bibliography of the Writings of Bret Harte in the Magazines and Newspapers of California, 1857–1871.* UCPES, 3(1933): 119–170.

Text

8   *The Writings of Bret Harte.* 20 vols. New York, 1896–1914.

Biographies

9   O'CONNOR, R. *Bret Harte, A Biography.* Boston, 1966.
10   STEWART, G. R. *Bret Harte: Argonaut and Exile.* Boston, 1931.

Critical Studies

11   BOOTH, B. A. "Bret Harte Goes East: Some Unpublished Letters." *AL*, 19(1948):318–335.
12   DUCKETT, M. *Mark Twain and Bret Harte.* Norman, Okla., 1964.
13   ERSKINE, J. *Leading American Novelists.* New York, 1910. (On Harte's short stories.)
14   HARRISON, J. B., ed. *Bret Harte: Representative Selections.* New York, 1941. (Useful for long introduction and critically annotated bibliography.)
15   HOWELLS, W. D. *Heroines of Fiction.* New York, 1903.
16   STEGNER, Wallace, ed. *Harte's "The Outcasts of Poker Flat" and Other Tales.* New York, 1961.
17   WILLIAMS, S. T. "Ambrose Bierce and Bret Harte." *AL*, 17(1945):173–180.

Sarah Orne Jewett (*1849–1909*)

Bibliographies

1 CARY, Richard. "Sarah Orne Jewett. . . ." *ALR*, 1(1967):61–66.
2 WEBER, Clara C. and Carl J. *A Bibliography of the Published Writings of Sarah Orne Jewett.* Waterville, Me., 1949.

Texts

3 Beyond her novels, her collections of short stories include: *Deephaven*, 1877; *Old Friends and New*, 1879; *Country By-Ways*, 1881; *A White Heron and Other Stories*, 1886; *The King of Folly Island and Other People*, 1888; *A Native of Winby, and Other Tales*, 1893; *The Country of the Pointed Firs and Other Stories*, 1896; *The Queen's Twin, and Other Stories*, 1899.
4 *The Best Stories of Sarah Orne Jewett.* Ed. with Introduction by Willa Cather. 2 vols. Boston, 1925.

Biographies and Critical Studies

5 BISHOP, Ferman. *The Sense of the Past in Sarah Jewett.* Wichita, Kan., 1959.
6 CARY, Richard. *Sarah Orne Jewett.* New York, 1962. (Includes up-to-date bibliography.)†
7 CHAPMAN, Edward M. "The New England of Sarah Orne Jewett." *YR*, 3(1913):157–172.
8 EAKIN, P. J. "Sarah Orne Jewett and the Meaning of Country Life." *AL*, 38(1967):508–531.
9 "Jewett Issue." *Colby Library Quarterly*, Ser. VI, No. X (June, 1964). (Essays by various critics, with bibliography.)
10 MATTHIESSEN, F. O. *Sarah Orne Jewett.* Boston, 1929.
11 THOMPSON, Charles M. "The Art of Miss Jewett." *AtlM*, 94(1904): 485–497.

Jack London (*1876–1916*)

Bibliographies

12 HAYDOCK, James. "Jack London: A Bibliography of Criticism." *BB*, 23(1960):42–46.
13 WALKER, Dale L. "Jack London. . . ." *ALR*, 1(1967):71–78.
14 WOODBRIDGE, H. C., John London, and G. H. Tweney. *Jack London: A Bibliography.* Georgetown, Calif., 1966. (Part Two includes studies about London, including reviews and dissertations.)

Biographies

1 FONER, Philip S. *Jack London, American Rebel.* New York, 1947.
2 HENDRICKS, King, and Irving SHEPARD, eds. *Letters from Jack London.* . . . New York, 1965.
3 LONDON, Charmian K. *The Book of Jack London.* 2 vols. New York, 1921.
4 LONDON, Joan. *Jack London and His Times: An Unconventional Biography.* New York, 1939.
5 O'CONNOR, Richard. *Jack London: A Biography.* Boston, 1964.
6 STONE, Irving. *Sailor on Horseback: The Biography of Jack London.* Cambridge, Mass., 1938.†

Critical Studies

7 BASKETT, Sam S. "Jack London and the Oakland Waterfront." *AL,* 27(1955):363–371.
8 BASKETT, Sam S. "Jack London's Heart of Darkness." *AQ,* 10(1958): 66–67.
9 BYKOV, Vil. "Jack London in the Soviet Union." *QNL,* 24(1959),52–58.
10 FRANK, Waldo. *Our America.* New York, 1919.
11 GEISMAR, Maxwell. *Rebels and Ancestors.* Boston, 1953.†
12 HENDRICKS, King. *Jack London: Master Craftsman of the Short Story.* Logan, Utah, 1966.
13 HOFFMAN, Frederick J. *The Modern Novel in America.* Chicago, 1956.†
14 JOHNSON, Martin E. *Through the South Seas with Jack London.* New York, 1913.
15 LABOR, Earle. "A Dedication to the Memory of Jack London." *A&W,* 6(1964):92–96.
16 LABOR, Earle. "Introduction" to *The Great Short Stories of Jack London.* New York, 1965.
17 LERNER, Max. "Introduction" to London's *The Iron Heel* [1906]. New York, 1957.†
18 LONDON, Charmian K. *The Log of the Snark.* New York, 1915.
19 LONDON, Charmian K. *Our Hawaii.* New York, 1917.
20 LYNN, Kenneth S. *The Dream of Success.* Boston, 1955.
21 MENCKEN, H. L. *Prejudices: First Series.* New York, 1919.
22 MILLS, Gordon. "Jack London's Quest for Salvation." *AQ,* 7(1955):3–14.
23 MILLS, Gordon. "The Symbolic Wilderness: James Fenimore Cooper and Jack London." *NCF,* 13(1959):329–340.

1   MORRELL, Ed. *The Twenty-Fifth Man: The Strange Story of Ed. Morrell, the Hero of Jack London's "Star Rover."* Montclair, N.J., 1924.

2   NOEL, Joseph. *Footloose in Arcadia: A Personal Record of Jack London, George Sterling, Ambrose Bierce.* New York, 1940.

3   O'BRIEN, Edward J. *The Advance of the American Short Story.* New York, 1923.

4   PATTEE, Fred Lewis. *The Development of the American Short Story: An Historical Survey.* New York, 1923.

5   PATTEE, Fred Lewis. *Side-Lights on American Literature.* New York, 1922.

6   PAYNE, Edward Biron. *The Soul of Jack London.* Kingsport, Tenn., 1933.

7   SINCLAIR, Upton. *Mammonart: An Essay in Economic Interpretation.* Pasadena, Calif., 1925.

8   WALCUTT, Charles Child. *American Literary Naturalism: A Divided Stream.* Minneapolis, 1956.

9   WHIPPLE, T. K. *Study Out the Land.* Berkeley, Calif., 1943.

10   WOODWARD, Robert H. "Jack London's Code of Primitivism." *Folio*, 18(May, 1953):39–44.

11   ZIRKLE, Conway. *Evolution, Marxian Biology, and the Social Sciences.* Philadelphia, 1959.

Joaquin Miller (1837–1913)

Texts

12   *The Complete Poetical Works of Joaquin Miller.* 6 vols. San Francisco, 1909–1910. (In 1915 another volume was added containing *The Building of the City Beautiful*, in prose.)

13   *Poetical Works of Joaquin Miller.* Ed. with Introduction and Notes by Stuart P. Sherman. New York, 1923.

Biographies

14   GOHDES, Clarence, ed. "Some Letters of Joaquin Miller to Lord Houghton." *MLQ*, 3(1942):297–306.

15   PETERSON, Martin S. *Joaquin Miller: Literary Frontiersman.* Stanford, Calif., 1937.

16   RICHARDS, John S., ed. *Joaquin Miller: His California Diary* [1855–1857]. Seattle, 1936.

Critical Studies

17   FROST, O. W. *Joaquin Miller.* New York, 1967. (Includes Bibliography.)

1 GOHDES, Clarence. *Literature of the American People.* Ed. by A. H. Quinn. New York, 1951.
2 "Joaquin Miller Memorial Number." *Overland Monthly,* n.s., 75(1920): 93–148.
3 TURNER, Arlin. "Joaquin Miller in New Orleans." *LHQ,* 22(1939): 216–225.

William Vaughn Moody (1869–1910)

Bibliography

4 HENRY, D. D. "Bibliography." In *William Vaughn Moody: A Study.* Boston, 1934.

Texts

5 Moody's major writings are: *The Masque of Judgment,* 1900; *Poems,* 1901; *The Fire-Bringer,* 1904; *The Great Divide: A Play,* 1909; *The Faith Healer,* 1909; *Some Letters of William Vaughn Moody,* ed. by D. G. Mason, 1913; *Letters to Harriet,* ed. by Percy MacKaye, 1935.
6 *The Complete Poetical Works of John Milton.* Ed. by William Vaughn Moody. Boston, 1899.
7 *The Poems and Plays of William Vaughn Moody.* Ed. by J. M. Manly. 2 vols. Boston, 1912.
8 *A History of English Literature.* (With Robert Morss Lovett.) Rev. ed. New York, 1918.†

Biographies

9 HENRY, D. D. *William Vaughn Moody: A Study.* Boston, 1934.
10 LOVETT, R. M. "Introduction." In *Selected Poems of William Vaughn Moody.* Boston, 1931.

Critical Studies

11 ADKINS, N. F. "The Poetic Philosophy of William Vaughn Moody." *TexR,* 9(1924):97–112.
12 BLACKMUR, R. P. "Moody in Retrospect." *Poetry,* 38(1931):331–337.
13 BUCKHAM, J. W. "The Doubt and Faith of William Vaughn Moody." *HomR,* 85(1918):349–353.
14 CARY, Richard. "Robinson on Moody." *CLQ,* 6(1962):176–183.
15 JONES, Howard M. "The Poet." In *The Bright Medusa.* Urbana, Ill., 1952.
16 JONES, Howard M. "William Vaughn Moody: An American Milton." *DD,* 4(1922):79–86.

1 KREYMBORG, Alfred. *Our Singing Strength: An Outline of American Poetry (1620–1930)*. New York, 1929.
2 LEWIS, C. M. "William Vaughn Moody." *YR*, 2(1913):688–703.
3 MATTHIESSEN, F. O. "William Vaughn Moody." In *The Responsibilities of the Critic: Essays and Reviews*. New York, 1952.
4 RIGGS, Thomas, Jr. "Prometheus 1900." *AL*, 22(1951):399–423.
5 WEIRICK, Bruce. "William Vaughn Moody, Nationalist and Mystic." In *From Whitman to Sandburg in American Poetry: A Critical Survey*. New York, 1924.

John Muir (1838–1914)

Texts

6 *Works*. Ed. by William Frederick Bade. The Sierra Edition. 10 vols. Boston, 1915–1924.
7 *Letters to a Friend*. Ed. by Jeanne C. Carr. Boston, 1915. (Muir's Letters to Mrs. Carr, 1866–1879.)
8 *John of the Mountains: The Unpublished Journals of John Muir*. Ed. by Linnie Marsh Wolfe. Boston, 1938.
9 *Studies in the Sierra*. Ed. by William E. Colby. San Francisco, 1950.

Biographies

10 JOHNSON, Robert U. *Remembered Yesterdays*. Boston, 1923.
11 WOLFE, Linnie M. *Son of the Wilderness: The Life of John Muir*. New York, 1945.
12 YOUNG, Samuel H. *Alaska Days with John Muir*. New York, 1915.

Critical Studies

13 FOERSTER, Norman. *Nature in American Literature*. New York, 1923.
14 HADLEY, Edith J. "John Muir's Views of Nature and Their Consequences." Ph. D. dissertation, University of Wisconsin, 1956.
15 JAMES, G. W. "John Muir: Geologist, Explorer, Naturalist." *Craftsman*, 7(1905):637–667.
16 MERRIAM, C. Hart, ed. *The Harriman Alaska Expedition*. 14 vols. New York, 1901.
17 SMITH, Herbert. *John Muir*. New York, 1965.†
18 TEALE, E. W., ed. *The Wilderness World of John Muir*. Boston, 1954. (An anthology, with much commentary.)
19 THAYER, J. B. *A Western Journey with Mr. Emerson*. Boston, 1884.†

Thomas Nelson Page (1853–1922)

Texts

1 *The Novels, Stories, and Poems of Thomas Nelson Page.* Plantation Edition. 18 vols. New York, 1906–1918.

Biography

2 PAGE, Roswell. *Thomas Nelson Page: A Memoir of a Virginia Gentleman.* New York, 1923.

Critical Studies

3 GROSS, Theodore L. *Thomas Nelson Page.* New York, 1967.
4 GROSS, Theodore L. "Thomas Nelson Page: Creator of a Virginia Classic." *GaR*, 20(1966):338–351.
5 HUBBELL, J. B. *The South in American Literature, 1607–1900.* Durham, N.C., 1954.
6 NELSON, John H. *The Negro Character in American Literature.* Lawrence, Kan., 1926.
7 QUINN, Arthur Hobson. *American Fiction: An Historical and Critical Survey.* New York, 1936. [Includes short stories.]
8 WILSON, Edmund. *Patriotic Gore.* New York, 1962.†

Francis Parkman (1823–1893)

Texts

9 *Francis Parkman's Works.* Frontenac Edition. 16 vols. New York, 1915.
10 *Francis Parkman: Representative Selections.* Ed. by Wilbur L. Schramm. New York, 1938.
11 *The Journals of Francis Parkman.* Ed. by Mason Wade. 2 vols. New York, 1947.
12 *The Letters of Francis Parkman.* Ed. with Introduction by Wilbur Jacobs. 2 vols. Norman, Okla., 1960.
13 *The Oregon Trail.* Ed. with Introduction and notes on variant readings by Elmer N. Feltskog. Madison, Wis., 1969.

Biographies

14 BASSETT, John S. "Francis Parkman, the Man." *SR*, 10(1902):285–301.

1 DOUGHTY, Howard. *Francis Parkman*. New York, 1962.
2 FARNHAM, Charles H. *A Life of Francis Parkman*. Boston, 1901.
3 FROTHINGHAM, Octavius Brooks. "Memoir of Francis Parkman." *PMHS*, 2nd ser. 8(1894):520–560.
4 SEDGWICK, Henry Dwight. *Francis Parkman*. Boston, 1904.
5 WADE, Mason. *Francis Parkman: Heroic Historian*. New York, 1942.
6 WHEELWRIGHT, Edward. "Memoir of Francis Parkman." *PCSM*, 1(1894):304–350.

Critical Studies

7 ALVORD, Clarence W. "Francis Parkman." *Nation*, 117(1923):394–396.
8 CASGRAIN, Henri R. "Biographies Canadiennes." In *Oeuvres Completes*, Vol. 2. Quebec, 1875.
9 DeVOTO, Bernard. "The Editor's Easy Chair." *Harpers*, 198(1949):52–55.
10 ECCLES, W. J. "The History of New France According to Francis Parkman." *WMQ*, 18(1961):163–175.
11 FAUTEUX, Aegidus. "Francis Parkman." *BRH*, 31(1925):177–183.
12 FISKE, John. *A Century of Science and Other Essays*. Boston, 1899.
13 HART, James D. "Patrician Among Savages: Francis Parkman's *The Oregon Trail*." *GaR*, 10(1956):69–73.
14 JACOBS, Wilbur. "Highlights of Parkman's Formative Period." *PHR*, 27(1958):149–158.
15 JACOBS, Wilbur. "Some of Parkman's Literary Devices." *NEQ*, 31(1958): 244–252.
16 JACOBS, Wilbur. "Some Social Ideas of Francis Parkman." *AQ*, 9(1957): 387–397.
17 KRAUS, Michael G. *A History of American History*. New York, 1937.
18 LEVIN, David. *History as Romantic Art: Bancroft, Prescott, Motley, and Parkman*. Stanford, Calif., 1959.†
19 MACY, John, ed. *American Writers on American Literature*. New York, 1931.
20 MORISON, Samuel E. "Introduction." In Parkman's *The Conspiracy of Pontiac*. New York, 1962.†
21 NYE, Russel B. "Parkman, Red Fate, and White Civilization." In *Essays on American Literature in Honor of Jay B. Hubbell*. Durham, N.C., 1967.
22 PEASE, Otis A. *Parkman's History: The Historian as Literary Artist*. New Haven, 1963.
23 PECKHAM, Howard H. "The Sources and Revisions of Parkman's Pontiac." *PBSA*, 37(1943):293–307.

1 PERRY, Bliss. "Some Personal Qualities of Parkman." *YR*, n.s. 8(1923): 443–448.
2 SHAFER, Joseph. "Francis Parkman, 1823–1923." *MVHR*, 10(1934):351–364.
3 TAYLOR, William R. "A Journey into the Human Mind: Motivation in Francis Parkman's *La Salle*." *WMQ*, 19(1962):220–237.
4 WINSOR, Justin. "Francis Parkman." *AtlM*, 73(1804):660–664.
5 WISH, Harvey. *The American Historian*. New York, 1960.
6 WRONG, George M. "Francis Parkman." *CHR*, 4(1932):289–303.

William Hickling Prescott (1796–1859)

Texts

7 *The Works of William H. Prescott*. Ed. by W. H. Munro. Montezuma Edition. Philadelphia, 1904.
8 *The Correspondence of William Hickling Prescott, 1883–1847*. Ed. by Roger Wolcott. Boston, 1925.
9 *Prescott: Unpublished Letters to Gayangos in the Library of the Hispanic Society of America*. Ed. by Clara Louisa Penney. New York, 1927.
10 *William Hickling Prescott: Representative Selections*. Ed. by William Charvat and Michael Kraus. New York, 1943.
11 *The Papers of William Hickling Prescott*. Ed. by C. Harvey Gardiner. Urbana, Ill., 1964.

Biographies

12 [Eulogies of Prescott]. *PMHS*, 4(1858–1860):167–196.
13 OGDEN, Rollo. *William Hickling Prescott*. Boston, 1904.
14 PECK, Harry T. *William Hickling Prescott*. New York, 1905.
15 TICKNOR, George. *Life of William Hickling Prescott*. Boston, 1864.

Critical Studies

16 BROOKS, Van Wyck. *The Flowering of New England*. New York, 1936.†
17 CHARVAT, William, and Michael KRAUS. "Introduction." In *William Hickling Prescott: Representative Selections*. New York, 1943.
18 CLARK, Harry H. "Literary Criticism in the *North American Review*, 1815–1835." *TWA*, 32(1940):299–350. (Summaries of many of Prescott's critical essays collected in 1850 as *Biographical and Critical Miscellanies*.)
19 LEVIN, David. *History as Romantic Art: Bancroft, Prescott, Motley, and Parkman*. Stanford, Calif., 1959.†

1   MORISON, S. E. "Prescott: The American Thucydides." *AtlM*, 200(1957): 165–172.

2   RINGE, Donald A. "The Artistry of Prescott's *The Conquest of Mexico*." *NEQ*, 26(1953):454–476.

3   WISH, Harvey. *The American Historian*. New York, 1960.

George Santayana (*1863–1952*)

Texts

4   *The Works of George Santayana*. Triton Edition. 14 vols. New York, 1936–1937. (Titles beyond technical philosophy most relevant to literature: *Platonism in the Italian Poets*, 1896; *The Sense of Beauty, being outlines of Aesthetic Theory*, 1896; *Interpretations of Poetry and Religion*, 1900; *Reason in Art*, 1905; *Three Philosophical Poets: Lucretius, Dante, and Goethe*, 1910; *Winds of Doctrine*, 1913.)

5   *Essays in Literary Criticism*. Ed. with Introduction by Irving Singer. New York, 1956.

6   *The Genteel Tradition: Nine Essays by George Santayana*. Ed. with Introduction by Douglas Wilson. Cambridge, Mass., 1967.

7   *Selected Critical Writings of George Santayana*. 2 vols. Ed. by Norman Henfrey. Cambridge, Eng., 1968.†

Critical Studies

8   AMES, Van Meter. *Proust and Santayana: The Aesthetic Way of Life*. Chicago, 1937.

9   ARNETT, Willard. *Santayana and the Sense of Beauty*. Bloomington, Ind., 1955.

10   GILBERT, Katherine. "Santayana's Doctrine of Aesthetic Expression." *PhilR*, 35(1926):221–236.

11   HOWGATE, George W. *George Santayana*. Philadelphia, 1938.†

12   KIRKWOOD, Mossie May. *Santayana: Saint of the Imagination*. Toronto, 1961.

13   LEAVIS, Queenie D. "The Critical Writings of George Santayana: An Introductory Note." *Scrutiny*, 3(1935):278–295.

14   MacCAMPBELL, Donald. "Santayana's Debt to New England." *NEQ*, 8(1935):203–214.

15   MILLER, Dickinson S. "Mr. Santayana and William James." *HGM*, (1921):348–364.

16   PRIESTLEY, John B. *Figures in Modern Literature*. London, 1924.

17   RANSOM, John C. "Art and Mr. Santayana." *VQR*, 13(1937):420–436.

18   RICE, P. B. "George Santayana: The Philosopher as Poet." *KR*, 2(1940): 460–475.

1   SINGER, Irving. *Santayana's Aesthetics: A Critical Introduction.* Cambridge, Mass., 1957.
2   STALLKNECHT, Newton P. "George Santayana and the Uses of Literature." *YCGL,* 15(1966):5–18.
3   VAN DOREN, Carl. "The Tower of Irony: George Santayana." In *Many Minds.* New York, 1924.

William Gilmore Simms (1806–1870)

Bibliographies

4   SALLEY, A. S. *Catalogue of the Salley Collection of the Works of William Gilmore Simms.* Columbia, S.C., 1943.
5   MORRIS, J. Allen. "The Stories of William Gilmore Simms." *AL,* 14(1942): 25–35. (Fifty-eight short stories listed chronologically.)

Texts (Nonfiction)

6   *The Writings of William Gilmore Simms.* Centennial Edition. Vol. I: "Voltmeier; or the Mountain Men." Columbia, S.C., 1969. (Introduction and explanatory notes by Donald Davidson and Mary C. Simms Oliphant. Text established by James B. Meriwether. The first of a multi-volumed edition completed in accord with the MLA Center for Editions of American Authors.)
7   The prefaces to Simms' many novels often embody important statements of literary theory. See especially *Woodcraft,* ed. with Introduction by R. C. Beatty, 1961 (first issued in 1852 as *The Sword and the Distaff*). Also *The Yemmassee,* ed. with Introduction by Alexander Cowie, 1937, and by C. Hugh Holman, 1961.†
8   The principal nonfiction works are as follows: *Lyrical and Other Poems,* 1827; *The Vision of Cortes, Cain, and Other Poems,* 1829; *The Remains of Maynard Davis Richardson,* 1833; *Slavery in America,* 1838; *The History of South Carolina,* 1840; *Donna Florida,* 1843; *The Geography of South Carolina,* 1843; *The Life of Francis Marion,* 1844; *Grouped Thoughts and Scattered Fancies,* 1845; *Views and Reviews in American Literature, History, and Fiction,*† *First and Second Series,* 1845 (the First Series has been edited with Introduction by C. Hugh Holman, 1962); *Areytos; or Songs of the South,* 1846; *The Life of Captain John Smith,* 1846; *The Life of Chevalier Bayard,* 1847; *Lays of Palmetto,* 1848; *Supplement to the Plays of William Shakespeare,* 1848; *The Life of Nathaniel Greene,* 1849; *The City of the Silent,* 1850; *The Lily and the Totem,* 1850; *Poems Descriptive, Dramatic, Legendary and Contemplative,* 1853; *South Carolina in the Revolutionary War,* 1853; *The Sack and Destruction of the City of Columbia, S.C.,* 1865; *A Succinct Memoir of the Life and Public Career of Colonel John Laurens,* 1867; *The War Poetry of the South,* ed. by Simms, 1867; *The Sense of the Beautiful,* 1870.

1 *The Letters of William Gilmore Simms.* Ed. by Mary C. Simms Oliphant, Alfred T. Odell, and T. C. Duncan Eaves. Introduction by Donald Davidson; Biographical Sketch by A. S. Salley. 5 vols. Columbia, S.C., 1952–1956.

Biographies

2 BROOKS, Van Wyck. *The World of Washington Irving.* New York, 1944.
3 SALLEY, A. S. See *Letters* above.
4 TRENT, W. P. *William Gilmore Simms.* Boston, 1892.

Critical Studies

5 CURRENT-GARCIA, Eugene. "Simms' Short Stories: Art or Commercialism?" *MissQ*, 15(1962):56–67.
6 DUVALL, S. P. C. "W. G. Simms' Review of Mrs. Stowe." *AL*, 30(1958): 107–117.
7 GUILDS, J. C. "Simms' Views on National and Sectional Literature, 1825–1845." *NCHR*, 34(1957):393–405.
8 HIGHAM, J. W. "The Changing Loyalties of William Gilmore Simms." *JSH*, 9(1943):210–223.
9 HOLMAN, C. H. "The Influence of Scott and Cooper on Simms." *AL*, 23(1951):203–218.
10 HOLMAN, C. H. "Introduction" to his edition of Simms' *Views and Reviews in American Literature, History and Fiction, First Series.* Cambridge, Mass., 1962.
11 HOLMAN, C. H. "Simms and the British Dramatists." *PMLA*, 65(1950): 346–359.
12 HOLMAN, C. H. "William Gilmore Simms and the *American Renaissance.*" *MissQ*, 15(1962):126–137.
13 HOLMAN, C. H. "William Gilmore Simms' Picture of the Revolution as a Civil Conflict." *JSH*, 15(1949):441–462.
14 HUBBELL, J. B. *The South in American Literature, 1607–1900.* Durham, N.C., 1954.
15 KEISER, A. *The Indian in American Literature.* New York, 1933.
16 PARKS, Edd W. *William Gilmore Simms as Literary Critic.* Athens, Ga., 1961.†
17 PARRINGTON, V. L. *Main Currents in American Thought*, Vol. II. New York, 1927.†
18 RIDGELY, J. V. *W. G. Simms.* New York, 1962.
19 RIDGELY, J. V. "*Woodcraft:* Simms' First Answer to *Uncle Tom's Cabin.*" *AL*, 31(1960):421–433.
20 TAYLOR, W. R. *Cavalier and Yankee.* New York, 1961.†
21 THOMAS, J. W. "The German Sources of William Gilmore Simms." *AGAGC*, 1(1957):127–153.

1   VANDIVER, E. P., Jr. "Simms' Border Romances and Shakespeare." *SQ*, 5(1954):129–139.

2   WELSH, J. R. "William Gilmore Simms, Critic of the South." *JSH*, 26(1960):201–214.

3   WIMSATT, Mary A. "Simms and Irving." *MissQ*, 20(1967):25–37.

Edmund Clarence Stedman (1833–1908)

Texts

4   *Victorian Poets.* Boston, 1875.

5   *Poets of America.* Boston, 1885.

6   *The Nature and Elements of Poetry.* Boston, 1892.

7   *The Works of Edgar A. Poe.* Ed. with Introductions in collaboration with George E. Woodberry. 10 vols. Chicago, 1894–1895.

8   *The Poems of Edmund Clarence Stedman.* Boston, 1908. (Includes poem collected from 1860, *Poems Lyrical and Idyllic.*)

9   *Genius and Other Essays.* Boston, 1911.

Biography

10   STEDMAN, Laura, and George M. GOULD. *Life and Letters of Edmund Clarence Stedman.* 2 vols. New York, 1910.

Critical Studies

11   DeMILLE, George E. "Edmund Clarence Stedman, Arbiter of the Nineties." *PMLA*, 41(1926):756–766. Repr. in DeMille's *Literary Criticism in America.* New York, 1931.

12   MARTIN, Jay. *Harvests of Change: American Literature, 1865–1914.* Englewood Cliffs, N.J., 1967.

13   PRITCHARD, John P. *Return from the Fountains.* Durham, N.C., 1942.

14   THORP, Willard. "Defenders of Ideality." In *Literary History of the United States,* ed. Robert Spiller and others. New York, 1948.

Henry Timrod (1828–1867)

Bibliography

15   SHEPHERD, H. E. "Henry Timrod: Literary Estimate and Bibliography." *PSHA*, 3(1899):267–280.

Texts

1   *The Poems of Henry Timrod.* Ed. by Paul H. Hayne. New York, 1873.
2   *Poems of Henry Timrod* [Memorial volume, based on the Hayne edition]. Boston, 1899.

Biographies

3   HUBBELL, J. B. *The Last Years of Henry Timrod: 1864–1867.* Durham, N.C., 1941.
4   THOMPSON, H. T. *Henry Timrod: Laureate of the Confederacy.* Columbia, S.C., 1928.
5   WAUCHOPE, G. A. *Henry Timrod, Man and Poet: A Critical Study.* Columbia, S.C., 1915.

Critical Studies

6   FIDLER, William. "Henry Timrod: Poet of the Confederacy." *SLM,* 2(1940):527–532.
7   HUBBELL, J. B. *The South in American Literature, 1607–1900.* Durham, N.C., 1954.
8   PARKS, E. W. Introduction to *The Essays of Henry Timrod.* Athens, Ga., 1942.
9   VOIGHT, G. P. "New Light on Timrod's 'Memorial Ode'." *AL,* 4(1933): 395–396.

Constance F. Woolson (1840–1894)

Texts

10   Beyond her novels, Miss Woolson published the following collections of short stories: *The Old Stone House,* 1872; *Castle Nowhere: Lake-Country Sketches,* 1875; *Two Women, 1862,* 1877; *Rodman the Keeper: Southern Sketches,* 1880; *For the Major,* 1883; *Jupiter Lights,* 1889; *The Front Yard and Other Italian Stories,* 1895; *Dorothy and Other Italian Stories,* 1896; *Mentone, Cairo,* and *Corfu,* 1896.
11   "Some New Letters of Constance Fenimore Wollson." Ed. by Jay B. Hubbell. *NEQ,* 14(1941):715–735.

Critical Studies

12   BENEDICT, Claire, ed. *Five Generations (1785–1923).* 3 vols. London, 1929–1930. (*Constance Fenimore Woolson* (1930), the second volume, was reprinted in 1932 with additions, including a bibliography.)

1 BROOKS, Van Wyck. *The Times of Melville and Whitman.* New York, 1947.

2 COWIE, Alexander. *The Rise of the American Novel.* New York, 1948. (Includes short stories.)

3 HUBBELL, Jay B. *The South in American Literature, 1607–1900.* Durham, N.C., 1954.

4 JAMES, Henry. "Miss Constance Fenimore Woolson." *HW*, 31(1887): 114–115. Repr. in *Partial Portraits.* London, 1888.

5 KERN, John Dwight. *Constance Fenimore Woolson: Literary Pioneer.* Philadelphia, 1934.

6 MOORE, Rayburn S. *Constance Fenimore Woolson.* New York, 1963.†

7 PATTEE, Fred L. "Constance Fenimore Woolson and the South." *SAQ*, 38(1939):130–141.

8 PATTEE, Fred L. *The Development of the American Short Story: An Historical Survey.* New York, 1923.

9 QUINN, Arthur Hobson. *American Fiction: An Historical and Critical Survey.* New York, 1936. (Includes her short stories.)

10 RICHARDSON, Lyon N. "Constance Fenimore Woolson." *SAQ*, 39(1940): 18–36.

NOTES

132

INDEX

INDEX

INDEX

INDEX

INDEX

F—H

INDEX

H

INDEX

140

INDEX

INDEX

M

142

INDEX

INDEX

INDEX

INDEX

INDEX

INDEX